W9-AVZ-212

vintage fashion
knitwear

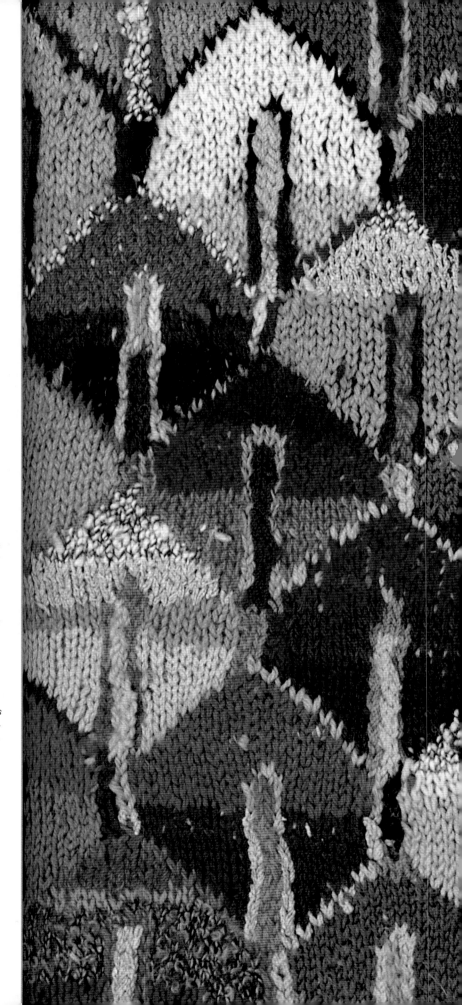

In memory of my father, Bert Fogg, an expert knitter.

Library of Congress Cataloging-in-Publication Data

Fogg, Marnie.
  Vintage fashion knitwear : collecting and wearing twentieth-century knitwear / Marnie Fogg. -- 1st ed.
     p. cm.
  Includes index.
  ISBN 978-1-60059-713-8 (hc-plc with jacket : alk. paper)
  1. Knitting. 2. Knitting--History. I. Title.
  TT835.F637 2010
  746.43'2--dc22
                                    2010017566

10 9 8 7 6 5 4 3 2 1

First Edition

Published by Lark Books, A Division of
Sterling Publishing Co., Inc.
387 Park Avenue South, New York, NY 10016

Published in 2010 by Carlton Books Limited
20 Mortimer Street
London W1T 3JW

Design and special photography copyright © Carlton Books
Limited 2010
Text © Marnie Fogg 2010
Foreword © Kaffe Fassett

Senior Executive Editor: Lisa Dyer
Managing Art Director: Lucy Coley
Design: A&E Design
Illustrations: Adam Wright
Copy Editor: Jane Donovan
Picture Researcher: Jenny Meredith
Production: Kate Pimm

Distributed in Canada by Sterling Publishing,
c/o Canadian Manda Group, 165 Dufferin Street
Toronto, Ontario, Canada M6K 3H6

Printed and bound in Dubai

ISBN 13: 978-1-60059-713-8

For information about custom editions, special sales, premium
and corporate purchases, please contact Sterling Special Sales
Department at 800-805-5489 or specialsales@sterlingpub.com.

For information about desk and examination copies available to
college and university professors, requests must be submitted
to academic@larkbooks.com. Our complete policy can be
found at www.larkbooks.com.

RIGHT A close-up detail
from Kaffe Fassett's Scales
waistcoat, 1970.

FAR RIGHT Carpet coat and
sleeveless sweater, from
Kaffe Fassett, 1983.

OVERLEAF A model wears a
green ribbed-knit bikini by
Cole of California in 1969.

vintage fashion
knitwear

*Collecting and wearing
designer classics*

Marnie Fogg

A Division of Sterling Publishing Co., Inc.
New York / London

Contents

Foreword
by
Kaffe Fassett

Knitting, after 40 years, is still mysteriously satisfying to me. To cast on and begin a swatch, exploring color combination or pattern structure, is as delightful as doing a jig or swimming in a summer pond. I suppose one of the things that keeps me so motivated is that I'm always building colors. Color has the power to heal our bad moods and keep us on a higher plane. My first sweater contained 20 new colors I'd just bought in the Scottish Highlands. As I built that first complex stripe I knew I was onto something life changing and indeed in the next years it overtook my painting career, leading to knitting books and working with the new up-and-coming Rowan Yarn Company. What put me temporarily on the fashion map was designing knitting for Bill Gibb and Missoni. Those were actually frustrating for me as machine-knitting was always highly limited in its use of color. In my hand bespoke knitting, I could use unlimited tones, often going up to 200 colors in a shawl or coat. My work has been purchased for several museum collections, which excites me as it means students of fashion can gain access to them. I'm also very enthusiastic about books like this. One that puts a designer like me in perspective with all the recent history of this humble but rewarding craft.

I make no apology for studying the past arts for inspiration. In my opinion there is nothing new under the sun. Good human design evolves from what each generation learns and teaches the next one. One of the most exciting inspirations was the costumes for Rudolf Nureyev's own production of the Romeo and Juliet ballet that featured rich red tones and voluminous sleeves.

When I started patterned knitting I was only interesting to a limited number of adventurous souls who rose to the challenge. Now knitting has become a tidal wave of enthusiastic practitioners who have experienced the buzz it holds. I'm sure those people who have only knitted the smallest scarf and sock projects but love the craft will graduate to more intricate fare. There is for me no better way to explore color ideas than to knit up units of tone in proximity. Seeing the rich collection of approaches in this book should inspire a whole new generation to pick up the needles and get stuck in.

RIGHT TOP AND BOTTOM
Two views of Kaffe Fassett's Romeo and Juliet coat, 1979, inspired by Nureyev's *Romeo and Juliet* ballet, which premiered at the London Coliseum in 1977. Knitted and modeled by Zoe Hunt, the sleeves and skirt are rendered in textured wools in rich tones, while a multicolored yoke is achieved in floral intarsia.

OPPOSITE A crewneck sweater inspired by Russian icons by Kaffe Fassett, 1993. The tesselated geometric pattern of outlined crosses has the simple flowing repeat of a weave draft, but the rich use of at least ten separate colors runs beyond the single repeat, creating unrestrained movement. The striped ribs are a classic, hand-knit Fair Isle detail.

'00s–'10s   '20s   '30s   '40s   '50s

Introduction

Everyone has a favorite sweater – there is something intrinsically comforting about the familiarity of donning a much-loved, much-worn garment that falls undemandingly around the body, providing both softness and warmth. It is no coincidence that knitted garments owe their provenance to underwear. Worn next to the skin, nothing caresses the body like vintage cashmere – it softens with wear and good washing.

Designers have deployed the diversity of the knitting process since hand-knitting became mechanized in the early years of the twentieth century. On the following pages you will find not only the fashions of the day, but the technological advances, the value placed on the handcrafted piece and radical new approaches to the singular stitch. More than any other fashion, knitwear is imbued with narrative and memory. The very act of knitting is a process invested with meaning; we learn the craft at our mother's knee and often attempt to wield the needles ourselves. Discovering vintage knitwear is a way of tapping in to other people's stories and making them our own, whether it is finding a precious beaded cardigan from the 1950s or a colorful 1980s Escada sweater complete with Velcro shoulderpads.

The processes of technical innovation and creativity are inextricably linked in designing fashion knitwear; the looped stitch can be fashioned into a myriad of shapes, structures and textures, setting trends, promulgating the avant-garde and providing red-carpet glamour.

In the beginning of the twentieth century, fabric manufactured on circular knitting machines introduced jersey into mainstream fashion, providing the modern wardrobe with ease, wearability and practicality. In 1916 Coco Chanel elevated this humble underwear material to haute couture status with her three-piece cardigan suits and set the paradigm for chic and stylish modern dressing. Hand-knitting introduced the Art-Deco-inspired jazz sweaters of the 1920s in strident patterns that reflected the hectic activities of the "flapper girls" as they dashed from dance floor to dinner party. Grown-up dressing in the more sober 1930s included the birth of the twinset, still a staple of every woman's wardrobe, produced in every sort of yarn from cashmere to cotton. During the rationing and deprivation of the 1940s, knitwear required innovation and ingenuity: old and worn-out sweaters were unraveled to form new ones, while short ends of yarns were incorporated in traditional British patterns such as Fair Isle. In America, the "Sweater Girls" posed and pouted for the troops, conical breasts encased in skintight knitwear. The cashmere cardigan emerged as a fashion frontrunner in the 1950s, worn in pretty pastels by day, and for evening, extravagantly embellished by Mainbocher and Helen Bond Carruthers. Neon outsize mohair sweaters and the perennial favorite of the Audrey Hepburn clones, the black turtleneck, featured in the wardrobe of the new phenomena: the teenager. Who hasn't admired Marilyn Monroe's way

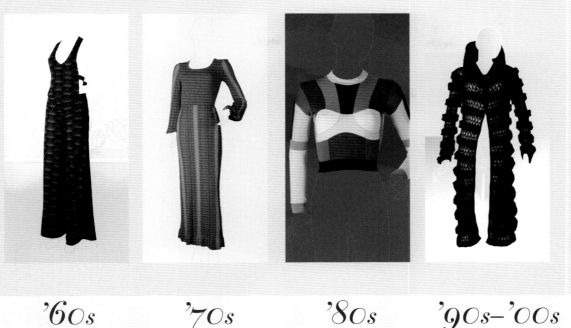

'60s   '70s   '80s   '90s–'00s

with knitwear in the 1960 film, *Let's Make Love*, when she clothed her curves in an outsize Aran sweater teamed with opaque black tights? Equally provocative were the untrammeled see-through crocheted and knitted minidresses of the 1960s, worn with kneeboots and little more than a smile.

The relationship between fashion and knitwear fluctuates in intensity over the decades, and in the 1970s the two came together with the refined, yet artisanal elegance of the Italian label Missoni. Influential entrepreneur Joseph Ettedgui and his label Joseph Tricot provided the metropolitan elite with their body-skimming knits and Martin Kidman produced the "big picture" sweater.

In the 1970s everyone tried the art of hand-knitting, inspired by the painterly knits of designer-makers such as Kaffe Fassett and Susan Duckworth. Tailoring was implicit in the term "power dressing" in the 1980s as women went to work in the trophy jacket and even their knitwear had shoulder pads. The Italian designers, including Krizia and Laura Biagiotti, emblazoned their knits with predatory animal patterns while American designer Norma Kamali undressed the gym-set with her sweatshirt collections.

Avant-garde designers, including Comme des Garçons and Rei Kawakubo, utilized the subversive properties of knitted fabrics in the minimalist 1990s. Invariably black, gray or navy, strange garments sprouted extra sleeves, controlled laddering and origami-like folds. Conversely, the velvet-trimmed cardigan, procured from Voyage, a shop that restricted entry to invitation-only, resulted in a wave of "bo-ho" copies when worn with bias-cut, printed tea dresses.

Vintage knitwear can evoke the lady-like decorum of the 1950s with a classic twinset, or images from the red carpet, as evidenced by the paparazzi frenzy over Julien Macdonald's sparkly, near-naked eveningwear. It may even be newsworthy: when First Lady Michelle Obama visited Europe in spring 2009, she wore a cardigan designed by Japanese designer Junya Watanabe to London's Royal Opera House. The asymmetrical garment with a panel of a fractured, deconstructed Argyle check, a pattern first utilized by Scotsmen in imitation of woven tartan socks, received world-wide coverage. Later the president's wife sported a cardigan by Azzedine Alaïa to meet Queen Elizabeth II at Buckingham Palace. American designer Oscar de la Renta was outraged at such informality, but it is evidence of how far knitwear has infiltrated not only mainstream, but high fashion, since its humble beginnings.

For those who are beguiled by the knitted stitch, whether handcrafted or machine-made, here you will find a plethora of information and images charting the changes in fashion knitwear from the Fair Isle sweaters of the 1920s to the rock-chick sweater dresses of contemporary designers.

1900–19:
From Combinations to Cardigans

With the arrival of knitwear into mainstream fashion at the beginning of the twentieth century, fashion finally became relevant to the lives of modern women. The unique properties of knitted fabrics, formed by the intermeshing of loops of yarn, rendered clothes form-fitting and yet unconfining, representing freedom for women from the rigid hierarchies and restrictive clothes worn before the First World War. Comfort and ease were not the prerequisite of Victorian and Edwardian dress; these attributes were only acquired with advances in knitting technology allied to the creative endeavors of designers.

The beginning of the twentieth century had been an era of ostentatious extravagance and conspicuous consumption. Women were clothed in sumptuous fabrics such as crepe de chine, *mousseline de soie* and embroidered brocade, all worked in the fashionable feminine hues of violet, pink and pale blue. Confined in the S-shaped corset, the entire body was concealed from the veil of the hat to the sweeping train of the skirt, collars were boned to the throat and gloves were worn up over the elbow. Contemporary couturier Lucille (Lady Duff Gordon) described the prevailing style:

> *For me there was a positive intoxication in taking yards of shimmering silks, lace as airy as gossamer and lengths of ribbons, delicate and rainbow-covered, and fashioning of them garments, so lovely that they might have been worn by some princess in a fairy tale.*

This ideal of Edwardian femininity was replaced by the colorful exoticism of Parisian couturier Paul Poiret, who created designs with great swathes of richly embellished fabrics and exuberant accessories of jeweled turbans and feathered hats. Although his influential Directoire line of 1908 discarded the corset, women were now literally shackled by the introduction of the designer's hobble skirt, which prevented the wearer from walking in any but the most timid steps. The segue from these complicated fashions to the understated pared-down simplicity of the 1920s that allowed women to walk freely was, in part, through the creative genius of Parisian couturier Coco Chanel and her innate understanding of the lives of modern women.

Undergarments and Outerwear

Hand-knitting became mechanized in 1589 with the invention of the stocking knitting frame by William Lee of Nottinghamshire. It was a process initially confined to hosiery, a definition that also included underwear. The majority of long-established knitwear manufacturers have their provenance in the production of underwear, including Jaeger. Knitted woollen underwear was regarded by dress reformer Gustave Jaeger as being essential for health. He believed that the wearing of undyed and knitted woollen fibers next to the skin would draw poisons from the body and allow it to breathe freely, and advocated the wearing of fitted woollen undergarments free of chemicals.

British knitwear company John Smedley, today a high-profile fashion brand, was founded in 1784 and manufactured "combinations" (also known as union suits), a conjunction of vest and drawers created in the 1870s. Long johns were an invention of the second John Smedley, who patented the method to make non-shrink underwear. Undergarments were also the products of knitwear company Pringle of Scotland. Their archives from the turn of the century show items for both men and women in their 47-page Winter Hosiery List, with lighter versions of the items being manufactured for the summer. Under menswear were listed shirts (vests), boys' dresses (combinations), trousers (long pants) and nightshirts, manufactured in a range of yarns, among them "Natural Cashmere and Fancy: Ribbed Cashmere; Elastic and Stout Merino; Spun Silk; and Silk and Wool." Listed under ladieswear were vests, dresses (combinations), drawers, cycle dresses, nightdresses and bodices.

In 1901 under the aegis of Robert Pringle, a lace edging was introduced to the tops of various items of ladies underwear, including vests, combinations and spencers. The spencer, or bodice, was initially worn for warmth under dresses. Now embellished with lace, it became an acceptable item of outerwear throughout the first decade of the century, a significant transition in the repositioning of a knitted garment from underwear into outerwear.

A hand-knitted coat or jacket occasionally replaced the jacket of the "tailor-made," a two- or three-piece suit for women in tweed, serge or linen, often constructed by tailors. These suits were worn in the country or when traveling, and by the minority of women who worked in offices as a sort of professional uniform. Pringle was eager to produce and market a machine-made version, and in 1907 two new items appeared on their hosiery list: "Knitted Blouses and Norfolk Jackets." A knitted coat department was formed in 1910:

We have pleasure in drawing the attention of our customers to the fact that we have now a very large and comprehensive range of the latest styles in high-class Knitted Coats. During the past year we have made this department a special study and have been obliged to greatly enlarge our factory to cope with the growing demand for these useful and handsome garments. In our range will be found all styles from Norfolk jackets to Steamer coats, beautifully finished and made in weights suitable for all requirements, and a choice selection of colourings embracing over fifty of the best and newest shades.

As the century progressed, knitwear manufacturers began to respond to the changing needs of their customers by moving production from underwear to outerwear, prompting both technological advances and, as knitwear became increasingly fashion-led, the necessity for a designer. The introduction of knitwear into mainstream fashion was one of the most significant innovations of twentieth-century dress.

RIGHT In this hand-knit underskirt in red and black wool, circa 1907–10, chevron stripes with relief welts are generated through repetitive "feather and fan" lace stitch on a garter-stitch base, The name of the owner appears on the inside waistband.

PAGE 10 This hand-knitted jacket, accessorized with a voluminous cable-knit beret and dating from 1915, recognizes the increasing informality and practicality of women's dress that took place during the period. The high V-neck is trimmed with a 1x1 button band.

OPPOSITE Knit manufacturers were discovering the power of brand marketing. Here a magazine advertisement for women's underwear dating from the early 1900s displays long ribbed vests with a popular coulisse ribbon trim.

MOST COMFORTABLE to WEAR

IN SILK, CASHMERE, COTTON & ALL KINDS OF WOOL.

THE "BOLTONIAN"

ELASTIC RIBBED

Under-Vest

ENGLISH MADE.

From Edwardian to Modern

The lavish luxury of couture houses such as Poiret, Doucet and Lucile now began to give way to the form and structure exemplified by Vionnet and Lanvin. In *The Age of Extremes*, historian Eric Hobsbawn cited 1914 as the point when "virtually everything that can take shelter under the broad and rather undefined canopy of 'modernism' was already in place: cubism, expressionism, futurism, pure abstraction in painting; functionalism and flight from ornament…"

Modernism offered a new aesthetic for a new century. A society reeling from the carnage of the First World War demanded a new set of values, ones that rejected the old established rules and social strictures, whether they concerned architecture, art or fashion. Viennese architect and essayist Adolf Loos denounced ornament a design crime. He wrote, "We are approaching a new and greater time. No longer by an appeal to sensuality, but rather by economic independence earned through work will women bring about her equal status with man. Then velvet and silk, flowers and ribbons, feathers and paint will fail to have their effect. They will disappear."

Knitwear fulfilled all the prerequisites of Modernism. Form followed function; knitted garments were adaptable to the seasons, light in weight and easily laundered. They allowed women not only freedom of movement but also, in a time of increasing female social mobility, released them from the constraints of high-maintenance clothes for the world of work. Fitness for purpose also included fashionable garments for the burgeoning interest in sports, and the emphasis that was placed on the body beautiful in the coming decade.

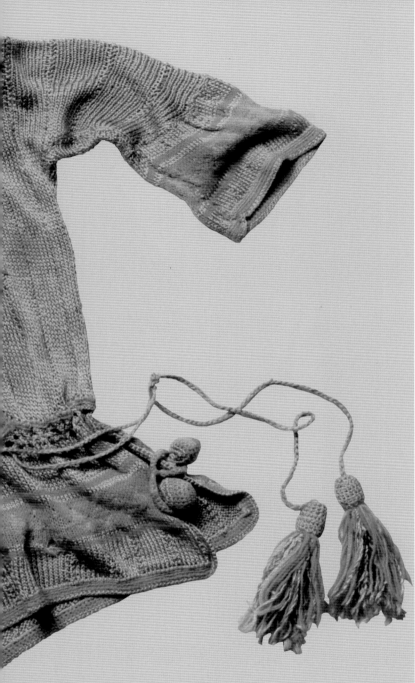

ABOVE AND DETAILS LEFT
Oriental extravagance in this
Poiret-inspired handworked
tunic in a lustrous ground
yarn with attached peplum
and tasseled coulisse. The
contrast diamond pattern
panels running vertically are
attached to the base fabric,
while the horizontal bands
are knitted in as
the panel develops.

LOOPING THE LOOP

Knitted fabric owes its flexibility to a loop structure which stretches and molds to fit body shapes. The interlocking of a series of loops, or stitches, is created either by hand or machine. The loops are interlocked using a needle to hold the existing loop while a new loop is formed in front of the old loop. The old loop is then brought over the new loop to form the fabric. Knitting differs from weaving in that a single piece of yarn can be used to create the entire length of fabric or garment. The fabric consists of horizontal rows known as *courses* and vertical columns of loops known as *wales*. Machine-knitted garments are either fully fashioned, or cut and sewn from a length of fabric.

Fully-fashioned knitwear

In 1864, William Cotton of England developed a machine to produce shaped garment pieces. This innovation propelled commercial knitting into an international industry. When knitting, increasing or decreasing the number of stitches in a row widens or narrows the garment being created. Increasing is achieved by moving outer loops sideways on a frame and creating extra loops. This process leaves a small eyelet hole in the fabric known as a fashioning mark. When decreasing, the process is reversed and the loops move inwards. This time the mark appears where two loops are compressed into one new loop. The final pattern pieces are sewn together by a process of linking, which forms a chain stitch on one side of the seam. Garments shaped in this way are known as fully fashioned and regarded as high quality. Occasionally some firms used fake fashioning marks to make garments appear to be fully fashioned.

Cut-and-sew knitwear (or cut-ups)

During the early nineteenth century, frame smiths began to make discoveries that paved the way for steam power to be applied to knitting technology. William Lee's frame required a sequence of horizontal and vertical moves to be made by the framework knitter in order to produce knitted goods. The automation of these movements was difficult, particularly when steam engines provided only rotary motion. However, Brunel, a French engineer and father of Isambard Kingdom Brunel, built a machine in 1816 that arranged the needles in a circular form rather than a flat bed. The machine produced a tube of fabric suitable for cut-ups, but it could not create fully-fashioned work. Circular knitting technology was further developed by Peter Claussen from Belgium, who patented an improved circular machine in 1845. It could produce a substantial tube of knitted fabric for cutting and was powered by hand or steam.

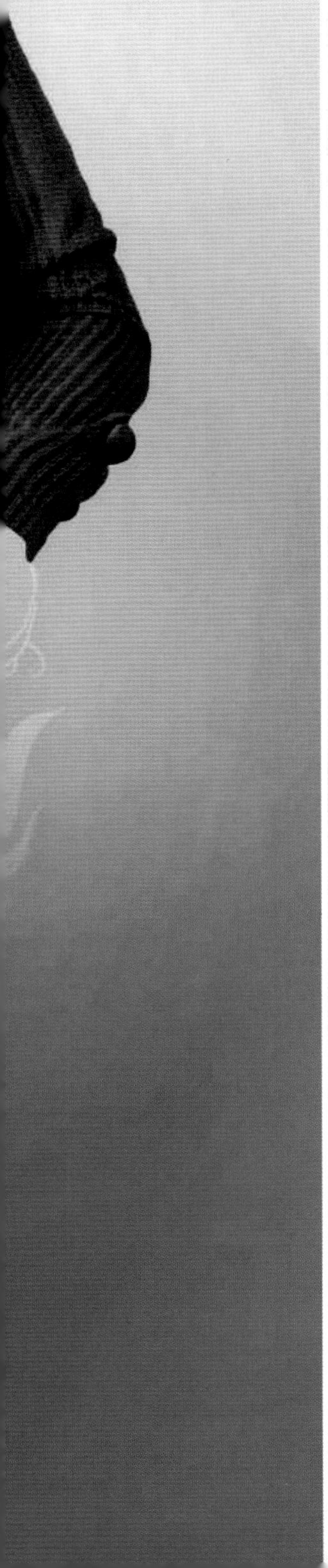

LEFT A softly tailored coat using "cut and sew" methods constructed from heavy single-jersey fabric in a two-tone vertical stripe. The military details of the sailor collar and turn-back cuffs show the impact of the First World War on fashionable dress.

RIGHT "Duster coats" were worn when driving in an open-top car and cut large to protect the clothes underneath. This knee-length version transforms the horizontal regimented weft stripes into bold vertical bands of color.

Coco Chanel

The most significant designer of the twentieth century, rivaled only a few years later by Elsa Schiaparelli, was Parisian couturier Gabrielle Chanel (1883–1971). (Chanel refused to acknowledge Schiaparelli's talent as a designer and always referred to her as "that Italian artist who's making clothes.") The two women had a formidable influence on contemporary fashion. Born in 1883 and raised first in an orphanage and then a convent, Chanel's aesthetic of pared-down glamour and apparent simplicity of style can be related to her upbringing. She claimed in 1914 that she was "in attendance at the death of luxury," a comment on the end of the *belle époque* and the true beginning of the new century.

Coco Chanel constructed her revolutionary functional clothes from jersey produced on circular knitting machines, developed by French textile manufacturing company Rodier. The designer rescued the fabric from warehouse oblivion in 1916 when she transformed the humble fabric, intended primarily for men's underwear, into a textile inextricably linked with twentieth-century style. Chanel understood the potential of this previously utilitarian fabric; reputedly so-called because its drape, movement and body-hugging properties had been appropriated by the *fin de siècle* femme fatale Lillie Langtry – the "Jersey Lily," who enchanted London society with her beauty and became the mistress of King Edward VII. A more likely but mundane explanation is that jersey is named after the sheep bred for wool on the island of Jersey.

Chanel used the fabric to fall loosely around the body, and her ideal shape was not the tortuous curves of the *belle époque*, but her own small-framed lithe athleticism. Gabrielle immediately adopted the fabric for herself, constructing an unbelted three-quarter-length overcoat totally lacking in embellishment and worn with a loose matching skirt. Cited with revolutionizing women's dress, Chanel transformed humble fabrics and practical shapes into fashion for the sophisticated urban woman. In her autobiography *Always In Vogue,* Edna Woolman Chase, editor-in-chief at *Vogue* from 1914–52, writes:

> By 1916 every Chanel day dress was jersey and the trimming was of rabbit fur … It was not long before she was established in the couture. Her jersey dresses, her sweaters, the magnificent jewels worn with the simplest of sports clothes created tremendous talk and became vastly popular.

Chanel's aesthetic, unique at the time, of simple, relaxed elegance with its roots in the utilitarian clothes of sport and leisure, was defined by the lifestyle of those who vacationed in the fashionable coastal resorts of the

French Riviera. With the assistance of her partner "Boy" Capel, Chanel opened a shop in Deauville, playground of the French elite; where from a small atelier she began making "off the peg" clothes. She attracted an aristocratic clientele more customarily used to buying couture; they were in part convinced by her own distinctive personal style, which included wearing a fisherman's jersey pulled in at the waist with a scarf. With her propensity for practical solutions and appropriation of working dress, couturier Paul Poiret named her style "poverty de lux."

Chanel's clothes particularly appealed to the athleticism of the American woman. Her first appearance in print was an illustration of a chemise dress from her Biarritz collection in *Harper's Bazaar* in 1916, the same year that she moved into her salon at number 31, rue Cambon. Chanel also designed the costumes for Serge Diaghilev's ballet *Le Train Bleu,* premiered by the Ballets

ABOVE Dating from 1904, this hand-knitted cable-knit sweater worn for golf is constructed to accommodate the restrictive S-shaped corset worn beneath.

ABOVE RIGHT In direct contrast, this 1910 photograph of French couturier Coco Chanel shows the designer exemplifying her personal aesthetic of comfort and simplicity in a loose-fitting, draped cardigan.

Russes in 1924 featuring hand-knitted bathing costumes, golf and tennis sweaters. Named after the train that travelled from the north to the south coast of France via Paris, the ballet featured bathing costumes such as those sold in her shop in Deauville, while the men wore plus-fours and knitted sweaters. The word "sweater" originates from around the 1880s, as its purpose was to absorb the sweat of exercise during sporting activities.

Women eagerly adopted Chanel's pioneering easy-to-wear fashion, and the three-piece knitted suit became a mainstay of every women's wardrobe. Comprising a cardigan (originally a front-buttoned loose jacket named after Lord Cardigan, who ordered it for his troops in the Crimean War), a skirt and a "pullover," so-called because it was literally pulled over the head, this aesthetic was perfectly attuned to the modern desire to appear fit, active and ready for the new century.

ABOVE A pink knitted swimsuit by Chanel for *Le Train Bleu*, choreographed by Nijinsky. Although these designs didn't appear until 1924, Chanel had already established her knitted sportswear in Deauville by 1914.

LEFT AND DETAILS RIGHT
Attributed to Chanel, and
dating from around 1918,
this loose-fitting, softly
tailored wrap-over jacket
closes with a low V-neck
onto a single button at
the dropped waistline; the
gathers are anchored by
a band of plain stocking
stitch sewn across the base
fabric. The combination of
"cut and sew" jacket with
matching skirt epitomizes
the new relaxed silhouette
introduced by the designer.
Embellishment is restrained,
limited to the Russian-style
embroidery on hem, cuffs
and collar.

▶ **Tennis cardigan**
Tennis cardigan
The elasticity of the basic loop structures of knitwear increasingly lent itself to the demands of sporting attire, and fashionable style became susceptible to expressing the physicality of sports. Here, champion tennis player Mrs. Blage wears her whites in Paris in 1912.

Key looks of the decades
1900-19

Jersey dresses and suits
Championed by Chanel, fine-weave jersey was used in day dresses and tailored suits and heralded a new casual approach to womenswear. Previously considered purely practical, jersey was elevated to haute couture, with apparel that was both beautiful and comfortable.

▲ **Hand-knitted suits**
A French-designed suit of fine hand-knitted rust silk comprising a long-line tunic top and ankle-length skirt. Contrast vertical stripes are punctuated with intarsia diamonds. The lace collar and cuffs are detachable for laundering and use on other garments.

Military influences
The war brought military detailing to knitwear, such as sailor collars, oversized patch pockets, stripes, rows of buttons and chainstitching, as well as shorter calf-length skirts and redingote jackets, all in color schemes of khaki, gunmetal gray and navy.

◄ Wool hats

As women discarded the formal attire of the Edwardian period, accessories became less ornate. This hand-knitted tam o'shanter beret, worn by Mrs. Hazeltine and dating from 1919, accommodates hair newly bobbed in the fashion of the day.

▼ Underclothing

The manufacturers of knitted undergarments in interlock and other industrially produced fabrics very often developed their businesses to include other items of apparel, eventually going on to produce knitted outerwear in the following decade.

▲ Exotic colors

Freed from the confines of the corset, the Oriental exoticism of this outfit from 1911 nevertheless inhibits the wearer's movement with the fashionable hobble skirt. The vibrant colors and patterning are resonant of the influence of the Ballets Russes.

1920s:
Jazz and the Sweater Craze

The radically simpler clothes of the 1920s introduced a fashionable body shape of svelte serpentine slimness based on the chemise, a straight low-waisted dress that hung from the shoulder and grew ever shorter as the decade progressed. This shortened skirt created a new erogenous zone, the legs, and kickstarted the global hosiery industry. Previously knitted on a circular machine and only steamed into shape, so that with wear they bagged at the knee and ankle, stockings now began to be fully fashioned. Made in two pieces and sewn together, knitted in beige or flesh-toned silk, the legs appeared thrillingly naked.

The newly tanned and worked-out body, fresh from the tennis court or ski slope, embraced this new near-nudity. The Modern movement demanded the pursuit of the perfect form and this included not only streamlining products and architecture, but also women's bodies. Hips and breasts were out of fashion; the *garçonne* silhouette perfectly suited a relaxed way of dressing that didn't differentiate significantly between active sportswear and daywear, particularly in America.

The loose flowing lines of the chemise appealed to the "flapper," a phenomenon of the decade, a notoriously free-spirited, young woman leading a hedonistic lifestyle supposedly predicated on high living and loose morals. In 1922 U.S. magazine *Outlook* printed an article by Ellen Welles Page, a self-confessed flapper:

> *I wear bobbed hair, the badge of flapperhood. I powder*
> *my nose. I wear fringed skirts and bright colored sweaters…*
> *I adore to dance. I spend a large amount of time in*
> *automobiles. I attend hops and proms; and ballgames*
> *and crew races, and other affairs at men's colleges…*

Informal Dressing

The new androgyny of silhouette resulted in the diminishing of the influence of the great Parisian couturiers such as Drecoll and Jacques Doucet, and even Paul Poiret found himself out of step with the current aesthetic of the time. Although Coco Chanel opened her salon in 1916, it was during this decade that she proved most iconoclastic and influential. In 1923 she met the Duke of Westminster, whose name was rarely mentioned without the soubriquet "the richest man in England." During their relationship Chanel purloined items of his sporting dress, sequestering tweed jackets, trousers and hand-knitted hip-length cardigans with roomy pockets, worn with hand-knit beige stockings.

This aesthetic translated in the summer to clothes that allowed for the new athleticism – tennis, golf, and horseback riding. Ironically, the leisure clothes of the aristocracy rendered fashion newly democratic. Three-piece cardigan suits did not require a ladies maid to dress the wearer; they were easy to manufacture and easy to copy. Speed was central to the age, mass production increased, and the fashion industry geared up to provide the new women consumers with their needs.

The informal way of dressing complied with the American fashion notion of comfort and ease. Although Parisian imports and Parisian copies made up the majority of high fashion in the prestigious department stores at the beginning of the decade, the proportion of American fashion in the shops had changed dramatically by the decade's end. New York designers such as Berthe Holley pioneered the concept of separates; a collection of interchangeable pieces comprising sweaters, blouses and skirts and the ever-popular cardigan jacket.

Chanel's jersey suits and beige tricot dresses were successful imports, as were Elsa Schiaparelli's trompe l'oeil sweaters and Jean Patou's golf ensembles. All the European designers understood the need to appeal to the American market, Patou going so far as to hire American models for his Parisian fashion shows. Knitwear included luxurious sports clothes such as angora cardigans and cashmere sweater ensembles by design houses such as Kurzman, whose exotic emporium, constructed from European castles, was sited on New York's Fifth Avenue.

RIGHT The geometric patterning of these three-piece cardigan suits dating from 1928 reflects the influence of the Art Deco movement. Use of broad striped trims to create decorative revers reinforces the architectural detailing produced by the striped cuffs and pocket edges.

OPPOSITE RIGHT AND BELOW Attributed to Chanel, this long loose cardigan with matching sweater uses a four-color stripe to create an undulating surface of light and shade. An early version of the twinset, it is produced by the "cut and sew" method, including a series of small dart suppressions at the nape of the neck.

PAGE 24 Gabrielle (Coco) Chanel exudes modernity in 1929. She wears a float-jacquard knit two-piece cardigan suit over a horizontally striped sweater with strands of pearls: components that formed the basis of the signature style that was to remain until her death in 1971.

BELOW AND RIGHT Mustard, cream and brown chevron-striped and belted tunic in racked half-cardigan stitch. The elongated shape is formed by the "cut and sew" method, with the hem and cuffs sewn by hand. A rectangular tortoiseshell buckle continues the geometric theme.

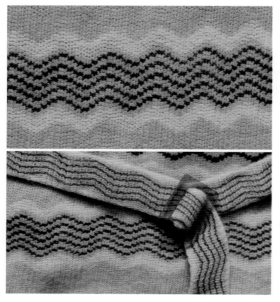

Art Deco and Cubism

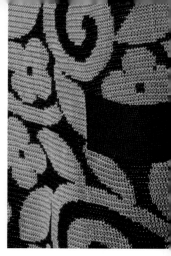

A generation of women brought up to provide garments for the armed forces during the First World War carried on knitting throughout the following decade, now using their skills to produce fashionable sweaters rather than serviceable socks. It was a decade dominated by youth and the "Bright Young Things." The hemline rose to unprecedented heights, freeing the body for the dance revolution of ragtime and jazz. In 1922 a leaflet by Weldon, publisher of *Practical Needlework*, featured patterns for "jazz jumpers," highly patterned and brightly colored hand-knit sweaters that reflected the artistic preoccupations of the time including the trapezoidal, zigzagged, geometric shapes, and the bold use of stepped forms and sweeping curves of Art Deco.

Art Deco originated in Paris, where it was called the Moderne, with the *Exposition Internationale des Arts Décoratifs et Industriels Modernes* (International Exposition of Modern Industrial and Decorative Art), although there had been some indications of the fragmented style before then. Paris, keen to promote itself as the global capital of luxury and style, was witness to the birth of a glittering and glamorous design movement that was to dominate decorative design over the next two decades. The movement peaked in popularity in Europe during the 1920s, but continued in the United States throughout the 1930s. It was inspired by various sources, including Constructivism, Cubism, Modernism, Futurism and the "primitive" arts of Africa, ancient Egypt and Mayan designs from Central America expressed in fractionated, crystalline, faceted forms.

The very nature of knitted fabric – its innate structure of horizontals and verticals – allowed for the geometric exploitation of color and flat planes and angles inspired by Cubism. Jean Patou produced sweaters (also called jumpers, from the French word *jupe*) featuring blocks of contrasting color and horizontal stripes inspired by the work of Pablo Picasso and Georges Braque. At the same time as Cubist works were being shown in Paris, artists Robert and Sonia Delaunay were experimenting with color in art and design, investigating a process called *simultanéisme*; simultaneous design occurs when one color is placed next to another, which is then "mixed" by the eye. Sonia's first large-scale painting in this style was *Bal Bullier* (1912–13), a work known for both its use of color and movement. Increasingly intrigued by the application of these principles to design, she extended her practice to include stage sets, furniture, fabrics, wall coverings and clothing. In 1924 she opened a fashion studio with couturier Jacques Heim; together they created a sensation with their Boutique Simultanée.

BELOW A "cut and sew" sweater in black and white jersey, banded with solid black knitted straps to match the asymmetrical neckline: the diamond effect was produced by laddering back the face loops of "normal" rib jacquard jersey.

ABOVE The design is produced by mechanical jacquard; each pattern row would require the perforation of an individual metal card or "steel" to correspond to the required selection.

OPPOSITE A formal kimono-style jacket evokes Oriental brocades with its stylized Art Deco florals. Two-color, striped back-rib jacquard forms the fabric structure – the same structure as demonstrated in the garment below, before it has been laddered.

THIS PAGE A knitted and embroidered jacket in black rayon or "art silk." Sumptuous beadwork in Chinese red bugle beads and metallic spheres lavishly borders every panel, recalling Oriental sources rendered into Art Deco motifs. The pattern is worked in a "vermicelli" cursive line.

LEFT AND DETAILS BELOW
Chinoiserie and other "Orientalist" themes were a popular subject for the embroidered embellishment that lent itself to the vogue for bohemian dress, an exotic element of 1920s fashion. Left, a black rayon-knit tunic dress with a contrasting panel of burnt orange. Throughout the garment, the bird and flower patterns are rendered by hand in delicate crewelwork.

RIGHT In contrast, this similarly styled knitted tunic dress is embroidered in an all-over repeat pattern of roses using a mechanical Schiffli embroidery machine. The large-scale industrial machine employs a form of pantograph mechanism to simultaneously sew cursive stitching in repeat along a length of fabric.

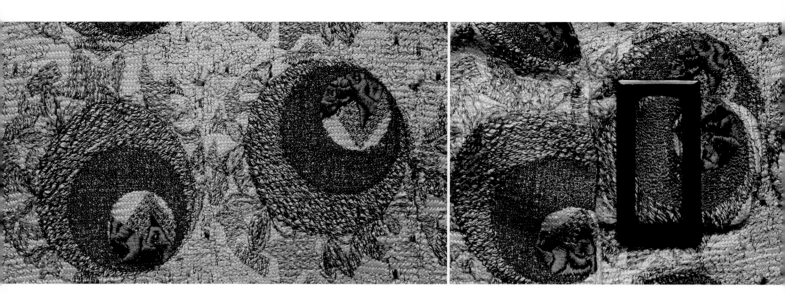

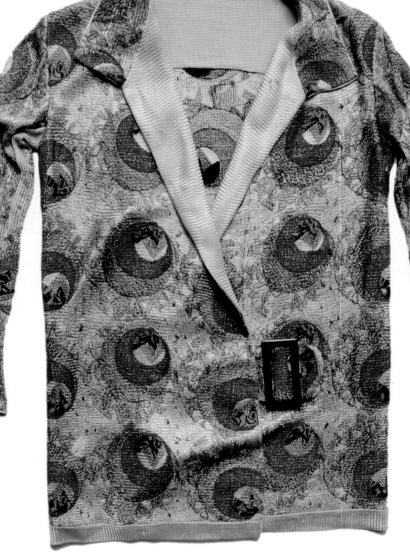

THIS PAGE An "Ottoman" semi-tailored jacket in cream rayon jersey. The opulence of the all-over embroidery, resonant of the floriated abstractions of Scottish designer Charles Rennie Mackintosh, renders the work as rich as a woven brocade. Use of Bakelite buckles at the waist and cuffs affirms the contemporary interest in this material.

Anyone for Tennis?

The exhilaration of being at peace sent the affluent classes into a whirl of sporting activity following the First World War. Polo, sailing, horse-racing and tennis became international events. "Sport has more to do than anything else with the evolution of the modern mode," said British *Vogue* in 1926, "there is only one thing of which everyone is convinced… and that is the perfection of adaption to the needs of a game which modern dress has evolved."

Opportunist manufacturers, aware of the marketing potential, exploited the market accordingly. New brand names like Superga, Dunlop and Slazenger supplied improved performance-wear, while luxury labels such as Louis Vuitton supplied the tennis clothes and Hermès the racket covers. René Lacoste, the French seven-time Grand Slam tennis champion, decided that the stiff tennis attire then worn was too cumbersome and uncomfortable for optimum performance on the court. He designed a white, short-sleeved, loosely knit piqué cotton (he called the cotton fabric *jersey petit piqué*) shirt with an unstarched, flat protruding collar, a buttoned placket, and a longer shirttail in back than in front (known today as a "tennis tail"), which he first wore at the 1926 U.S. Open championship.

In 1927 Lacoste placed a crocodile emblem on the left breast of his shirts, as the American press had begun to refer to him as "the Alligator" owing to his aggressive style of playing. Its sartorial rival, the polo shirt, was created in 1920 by Lewis Lacey, an Argentine Irish haberdasher and polo player. He produced a shirt that was embroidered with the logo of a polo player, a design originating at the Hurlingham Polo Club near Buenos Aires. The term "polo shirt," which previously referred only to the long-sleeved, buttoned-down shirts traditionally used in polo, soon became a universal name for the tennis shirt.

Tennis fashion for women included knitted sleeveless pullovers with ribbed welts in contrasting colors, the forerunner of the classic tennis and cricket sweater with its striped V-neck. The female body was now celebrated for its athleticism, and sporting heroines such as Suzanne Lenglen, known as the "Divine Lenglen," were the feminine ideal. A symbol of emancipation, Lenglen was as renowned for her fashionability as for her prowess on the court. The couturier Jean Patou was commissioned to design a pleated knee-length skirt and a sleeveless cardigan for her, and eventually he went on to establish a sportswear department in 1922, alongside couturiers such as Jeanne Lanvin and Jacques Heim.

RIGHT Daringly baring her arms in 1925, French tennis player Suzanne Lenglen helps set the trend for the new female archetype of fashionable athleticism. Her coordinated signature headband accessorizes the tunic dress and long, sleeveless knitted gilet.

John Smedley and the Isis Shirt

The 1920s heralded the production of British knitwear manufacturer John Smedley's most iconic garment, the Isis tennis shirt, a style subsequently known as the polo shirt (see a 1950s example of an Isis shirt on page 100). Attempts have been constantly made by other manufacturers to reproduce the unique collar of this sports shirt, patented as the "Vestee." This comprises not the usual two-piece placket but a single piece of knitted fabric that is attached to both sides of the collar, turning at the bottom to produce a flat three-button opening. Although initially worn for tennis, the shirt was produced in several colors. There are five machines unique to Smedley that are currently in use to produce both this classic style and one called Dorset.

The John Smedley company has been a family-owned business for 225 years, utilizing production methods and handcrafted finishing techniques that have been passed down through the generations while also exploiting modern technology. The factory was founded in 1784 by John Smedley and Peter Nightingale near Matlock in Derbyshire, England, 13 years after Richard Arkwright developed the first water-powered spinning mill in 1771 in nearby Cromford. Initially specializing in the production of muslin and spinning cotton, supplying outworkers in nearby cottages with yarn for their hand-frame looms, by the end of the eighteenth century the company had extended its activities to include knitting and hosiery manufacture within the factory system. When he died in 1875 the second John Smedley had no heir, and the business was passed onto a third John, a cousin J. T. Marsden Smedley, who after his death in 1877 entrusted the company to his son, the fourth John B. Marsden Smedley. He remained chairman for 70 years, installing up-to-the-minute knitting machines and forming a limited company in 1893. Production expanded to include underwear and knitted outerwear.

RIGHT A wool, plain-knit undervest with shoelace straps and a drawstring top by knitwear manufacturer John Smedley from the 1920s. The simple chemise shape reflects the prevailing style of the tubular figure-skimming fashions.

OPPOSITE As fashion became more form-friendly throughout the following decade, underwear reflected a greater body consciousness, seen here in a fine wool vest by John Smedley with fully-fashioned bra top from the 1930s.

John Smedley is renowned for knitting fully fashioned, fine-gauge products resulting in an ultra-lightweight fine knit, rarely produced by other manufacturers. The company's policy was described in a sales document in 1934:

It is as necessary to spin good yarn in fact as in fable, and the success of the manufacturer rests to a large extent on this knowledge. He must not only know the very source of his material but supervise each process it undergoes from the beginning…The best Australian lamb's wool, silk, cashmere and other fibres, are brought to Lea Mills, where each is treated and blended in the manner best suited to before being spun into yarns. There, they undergo the spinning, the proper doubling and twisting before all is ready for full fashioned knitting. The complete coordination between the departments – each so different, yet each in the same building – results in the achievement of the perfect blend of fabric appropriate to each type of garment. Our outstanding speciality is that the garments are mainly manufactured on the full fashioned frames, of which we believe we have the largest and the most up-to-date in the world.

The John Smedley company continued to manufacture both men and women's underwear in the 1930s, including the traditional combinations and directoire knickers in cashmere, angora and silk mixtures and the lighter spun silk, and the Milanese and Jaylax lace underwear. Women's petticoats now reflected the shapelier silhouette of the decade, having fully-fashioned bra tops. Not only were the traditional white and pink colors used, checks and stripes appeared on knickers and pants for men. Smedley's were also producing fashion-led knitwear. Matching cardigans and pullovers were more versatile than the simple twinset, the pullover featuring design details such as a collar and short sleeves. Underwear and nightwear began to evolve into leisurewear, with silk "Nightie-Pajamas with a matching Boudoir wrap" and fine rayon and wool mixture palazzo trousers with a pintucked waist and matching top of cap sleeves and bow.

Unlike Pringle, who exported chiefly to America, John Smedley exported to those areas with which they already had a trading relationship from importing silk and cotton: Burma, the Malay states, China, Japan, the Dutch East Indies, Siam, Australia, South Africa and Rhodesia, France, Italy, Belgium, Norway, Sweden, Denmark and Holland.

RIGHT Back view of a 1920s two-piece bathing suit by John Smedley. To enhance its functionality, the fabric is robust and relatively inelastic. The check effect is attained by crossing horizontal weft stripes with vertical warp stripes, introduced by "lace bars" and adding fine warp lines of color.

TYPES OF WOOL

Wool is the most commonly used yarn for knitted garments. For centuries, sheep have provided mankind with both food and clothing. Wool is durable, flexible and ecologically sound.

The quality of wool that sheep produce varies according to breed and location. Merino sheep, originally a Spanish breed, produce wool that is noted for its whiteness and fineness. Lambswool is wool sheared from a lamb between 11 and 12 months old, the first year clip. Merino comes from the second year clip and is considered the most valuable of wools. Australia produces about 43 percent of the world's Merino wool. Any wool taken from the sheep in subsequent years is suitable only for blankets and carpets.

Shetland wool is the clip of lambs from the Shetland Islands and North of Scotland, where the colder climate produces a heavier yarn.

United States sheep producers raise four breeds of sheep that produce fine wool and fifteen breeds that produce medium-grade and coarse wools. The medium-grade wool comes from breeds raised primarily for food. Although sheep producers exist in all States (except Hawaii), most sheep operations are in the West.

The Production Process

◆ **Shearing:** Sheep are sheared once a year, usually in the spring. The wool is trimmed in one piece, called a fleece.

◆ **Scouring:** The fleece is washed to remove impurities, such as dirt, grease and dried sweat. Impurities account for between 30 and 70 percent of the fleece weight. At this point, the wool is considered cleaned wool or scoured wool. The grease that is removed is considered a valuable by-product. Lanolin, in its purified state, is used in creams, soaps, lotions, cosmetics and ointments.

◆ **Dyeing:** In quality garments, the fleece would be dyed. In inferior-quality garments the color is added at the yarn stage.

◆ **Carding:** The wool is combed to straighten the fibers.

◆ **Spinning:** Once straightened, the fibers can be spun into yarn. The thread produced by a process of spinning is called a single yarn. This is unsuitable for hand-knitting. Two, three or four ends of a single yarn are twisted together to produce two-, three- or four-ply wool.

FANCY YARNS

A yarn is any kind of spun thread. Fancy yarns are yarns that differ from the normal construction by the deliberate introduction of irregularities such as knots, loops, curls, slubs, and so on.

Bouclé: Yarns with a twisted core with an effect wrapped around it so it produces the distinctive looped surface.

Chenille yarn: A yarn that has a cut pile consisting of a variety of fibers helically disposed around axial threads which secure it.

Crepe: A highly twisted yarn. Also moss crepe yarn, a two-ply yarn made by doubling a normal twist with a high-twist yarn.

Fair Isle Knits

Golf was the sport of choice for the Duke of Windsor, later Edward VII. When the Prince appeared in a Fair Isle sleeveless pullover while playing golf, the indigenous knitwear went from being a local speciality and tourist keepsake to the pages of the fashion magazines. He later recorded the event in his book, *A Family Album*: "I suppose the most showy of all my garments was the multicolored Fair Isle sweater with its jigsaw pattern, which I wore for the first time while playing myself in as Captain of the Royal & Ancient Golf Club at St. Andrews in 1922."

Originally found on the small Scottish island between Orkney and Shetland, Fair Isle sweaters were initially made to supplement the income from fishing and farming. It was a craft that needed little equipment and a skill that could be passed down the generations and was, at times, practiced by men and women alike. The earliest museum samples date from 1850, but the patterned knitwear was first mentioned by Samuel Hibbert as bright caps of "fantastical colors" worn by the Shetland men in his *A Description of the Shetland Islands* in 1822. Although travellers to the area noted multicolored gloves and stockings (socks) being worn by the islanders, there is no evidence of the sweaters being made before 1914.

The attention given to Prince Edward's sartorial choice led to a large increase in production on the island during the 1920s, when Shetland knitters then expanded their work to include hats, gloves and cardigans. The Fair Isle sleeveless sweater (later called a "tank top") became a vital item in the wardrobe of the male dandies of the era. Initially worn for sporting activities, the patterned sweater was seen on every fashionable undergraduate, worn with "Oxford bags," the wide-legged trousers that covered the shoes.

The earliest examples of yarn used for Fair Isle knitting were from the indigenous sheep of the island and left undyed in their natural colors of white, gray and brown. Later color was introduced by dyeing the yarn with various lichens. Yellow was produced from onion skins, and expensive madder and indigo were imported to the island to produce red and blue. Although traditional color schemes were yellow and white motifs on a ground of banded red, indigo and black, the 1920s propensity for beige resulted in the background colors generally being restricted to fawn, gray or "game-fleck," like the plumage of a partridge.

The typical patterning of the original Fair Isle was made up of horizontal bands of color, usually less than 15 rows deep. The separation of circular motifs by four diagonal corners produced the so-called OXO designs, the X with a vertical line running through its center. As time progressed, other motifs were added to the vocabulary of the knitters. Patterns often included symbols that held special meaning: the cross for faith, the anchor for hope and the heart for charity. The simplest method of

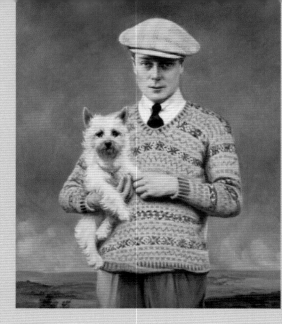

knitting a colored pattern is to work together two threads of different colors, stranding the unused yarn behind the working yarn at each stitch. No more than two or three colors can be used, as the strands would be too long for practicality. The resulting double thickness of a sweater knitted in this style provided ideal protection against the damp and cold of the northern European weather, being warm and flexible yet durable. Although production burgeoned during the 1920s, pattern books were rarely used until enterprising islanders, Mary Johnstone and her brother, produced graphs of the designs for commercial purposes in 1927.

Traditional Fair Isle sweater construction usually involves knitting the body of the sweater in the round, sewing or otherwise fastening the work securely where the armholes are to go, and then cutting the knit fabric to make the armholes. These cuts are known as "steeks" in American knitting technology but not in the Shetland Isles, where the Fair Isle technique was developed. This tradition and skill has been handed down from generation to generation. Although the term 'Fair Isle' is used to describe the style of pattern, true Fair Isle pieces are only knitted in the Shetlands. In recent years Fair Isle has inspired designs by Missoni, Ralph Lauren, Alexander McQueen and Burberry, though the yarn used is more likely to be cashmere than Shetland wool.

ABOVE A portrait of HRH The Prince of Wales from 1925 by John St. Helier Lander shows the Duke in his favorite jigsaw-patterned Fair Isle sweater.

RIGHT Men's sweaters showing variations in color and patterning of the Fair Isle knitting technique from the Fair Isle Knitwear Group, dating from 1920–30.

OPPOSITE TOP Vacationing socialite Miss Rachel Wallace of Boston, Massachusetts, signifies her leisure status at Hot Springs, Vancouver, by adopting the folk-patterning of a Scandinavian sweater. The look is rendered more urbane by the detachable linen collar and cuffs plus coordinated leather belt and correspondent shoes.

STITCH VARIATIONS

Cable stitch: Two or more groups of adjacent wales that pass under and over one another to give the effect of a plaited rope.

Intarsia: Weft knitted plain, rib or purl fabrics containing designs in two or more colors within the same course. Each area of color is knitted from a separate length of yarn.

Lace stitch: An openwork effect produced by transferring needle loops to an adjacent needle of the same needle bar.

Picot: In knitting, picot edges or hems are produced by making a row of lace eyelets in stocking or plain stitch and then making a fold of fabric with the holes along the folded edge, forming small scallops.

Racked stitch: A sideways deflected stitch that lies across a stitch formed in the same course on the opposite needle bed and has a ric-rac effect.

Raschel lace: Lace fabric produced on a raschel warp-knitting machine.

Space-dyeing: The production of multicolor yarns by applications of various colorants at intervals along a yarn, producing a multicolored fabric from a single thread.

Terry: Uncut loops in fabric, associated with towelling (terry).

Velour, warp knitted: A two- or three-bar warp knitted fabric in which a pile is produced. The fabric is trimmed after raising.

Elsa Schiaparelli

While Chanel designed wearable clothes of an easy elegance, her great rival, Elsa Schiaparelli, produced garments that challenged the wearer and combined the avant-garde with high-octane glamor. Born into a family of wealthy intellectuals, the designer was a close friend of the poets, philosophers and artists of the day including Salvador Dalí, Man Ray and Picasso. Her fashion was always concerned with ideas, while Chanel's aesthetic had much more to do with lifestyle. Schiaparelli's first excursion into design had an immediate effect. In the words of her autobiography, *A Shocking Life*, when she introduced her iconic trompe l'oeil bow sweater to Parisian society, she "created a furore. ...All the women wanted one, immediately."

Intrigued by the hand-knitted sweater of a friend, Schiaparelli continues to recount in her book how it had a "steady" look, and discovered that its firmer texture was the result of a technique deploying a three-needle stretch-resistant process, which produced a tweed-like effect. This was achieved by carrying the white yarn across the back of the black yarn and catching it behind every third or fourth stitch as it was being knitted. The technique was the work of Armenian immigrants, Arousiag Mikaelian and her brother, who produced knitted goods for the wholesale trade. Although Schiaparelli herself did not know how to knit, saying "the art of clicking those two little metal needles

and making them produce something has always been a mystery to me," she describes the collaboration with the knitters:

> I drew a large butterfly bow in front, like a scarf around the neck – the primitive drawing of a child of prehistoric times. I said, 'The bow must be white against a black background, and there will be white underneath.' The first sweater was not a success. It came out lopsided and not at all attractive. The second was better. The third I thought sensational.

The fashion editor of the December issue of American *Vogue* agreed, describing the sweater as a "masterpiece." The first order, for 40 sweaters with matching skirts, was completed in two weeks. Orders from American sportswear wholesaler W. H. Davidow Sons followed, and by 1928 the design was so ubiquitous that knitting instructions appeared in *Ladies' Home Journal* without attributing its source.

Copying was rife – Schiaparelli was not the only victim. Replicas of hand-knitted sweaters by Jean Regny and Lucien Lelong were advertised by Macy's in *The New York Times*. It was routine for a single garment to be purchased direct from the designer and then copied for the mass-production market at a greatly reduced price. However, Schiaparelli was resigned: "the moment that people stop copying you, it means that you are no longer any good and that you have ceased to be news." In 1928 *The New Yorker* confirmed that "Schiaparelli, after all, belongs to knitted sweaters, or they to her."

ABOVE The celebrated, best-selling sweater designed by Elsa Schiaparelli with a trompe l'oeil graphic bow at the neck. The bow is created using a classic Fair Isle structure, where any yarn not required in the face side of the material is carried across the reverse and caught into the back of the stitches to avoid long "floats." This technique forms a uniformly less elastic knit.

LEFT Parisian couturier Elsa Schiaparelli (1890–1973) photographed in the 1950s by Sylvia Salmi.

OPPOSITE A gray hand-knit sweater-coat with black bone buttons designed by Schiaparelli is modeled by Muriel Finley and photographed by Edward Steichen in 1928. The structured tailoring of the collar and patch pockets contrast with the soft, loose-knitted texture of the jacket, which is accessorized with a cloche hat designed by Rose Valois.

In 1928 Schiaparelli moved to 4 rue de la Paix, and erected a black-and-white sign *Pour le Sport* on the front door. From here the designer produced a collection of hand-knitted sweaters, coats, skirts, bathing suits and crocheted berets. Some sweaters utilized the new elastic woollen fabric, kasha, which clung provocatively to the body. The trompe l'oeil effects now included faux scarves, neckties and belts, and more avant-garde subject matter. She writes:

> *One was tattooed like a sailor's chest with*
> *pierced hearts and snakes. There was a skeleton*
> *sweater that shocked the bourgeois but hit the*
> *newspapers, which then took little notice of*
> *fashion. White lines on the sweater followed*
> *the design of the ribs so that women wearing*
> *it gave the appearance of being seen through*
> *an X-ray… and fish wriggling on the stomach*
> *for a bathing suit.*

The designer's innovations were not restricted to surface decoration. Her first patent was for a backless bathing suit that incorporated a brassière with straps that crossed low on the back and fastened in the front at the waist, made in a thick herringbone-striped knit. Schiaparelli had enormous international commercial success with a tiny knitted cap like a tube; the "madcap" could be pulled into a variety of shapes and, like the bow-front sweater, was copied in thousands.

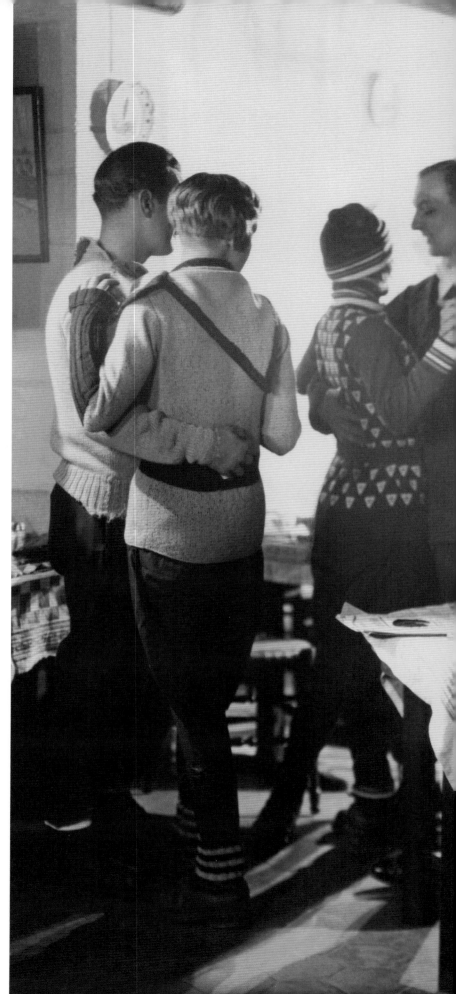

RIGHT Couples enjoy a late-afternoon après-ski dance in Switzerland, photographed by George Hoyningen-Huene in 1929. The skiing suit and belted sweater (left) were designed by Schiaparelli, while French couturier Jane Regny created the triangle-patterned belted sweater and knit cap (center) and military-inspired sweater with large buttons, belt and trim in contrasting color (right).

FABRIC TYPES

Cloqué fabric or blister fabric: A rib-based fabric with a relief pattern which may be a different color from the ground.

Double jersey (weft knitting): A generic name applied to a range of knitted fabrics made on a rib or interlock basis, the construction of which is often designed to reduce the "stretchability" of the structure.

Felted fabric: A fabric where the fibers have been matted together during the processing or in use.

Fleece fabric: A plain weft-knitted fabric with a ground yarn and in which a yarn of low twist, secured by a binder, appears on the back of the fabric and may be brushed or raised.

Laid-in fabric, weft-knitted: A fabric containing non-knitted yarns which are held in position by the knitted structure.

Plain fabric: A fabric in which all the component knitted loops are of the same kind and meshed in the same manner.

Plated fabric: A fabric knitted from two yarns of different properties, producing a reversible design.

Purl fabric: A fabric in which both back and face loops are in some or all of the wales, or rows.

Rib fabric: A weft-knitted fabric in which both back and face loops of the same type occur along the course, forming a strong elasticized edge to a garment hem or cuff.

Single jersey: A generic name applied to knitted fabrics made on a plain knitted base. In hand-knitting it is then called stocking stitch.

▶ **Unstructured style**
White silk knit-and-crochet dress for day dating from 1923. A crochet-edged boat neckline is teamed with a loosely draped fabric, structured by drawstrings at the waist. The silhouette of the open-sleeved tunic recalls the style worn for the fashionable "callisthenics" exercises, for which participants adopted a version of classical Greek dress.

▲ **Knitted jackets**
An integral element of every woman's wardrobe, the relaxed silhouette of the knitted jacket replaced the stiff tailoring of the tweed "tailor-made" of the previous decade. This illustration dates from 1924: the long, loose shape, roll collar and single button placing the emphasis on the hip are typical of the period.

Key looks of the decade

1920s

Beads and embroidery
Elaborate embellishment with embroidery and beadwork in Oriental and Art Deco motifs were a feature of knitwear design during this era, particularly for eveningwear. Ornate beadwork was also a feature of the decade's flapper dress, a short, sleeveless chemise.

◀ **Art Deco and geometrics**
A 1925 oversized twinset designed by Joseph Paquin. Bold crochet-knitted, multicolored chevron stripes are resonant of the influence of Art Deco. Both the seven-eighths-length coat and full-length dress have wide plain button bands from neck to knee.

The cardigan suit

This 1924 design by Jeanne Lanvin epitomizes the elegance and form of the outerwear of this period. The three-piece knitted suit of embellished long cardigan, narrow calf-length skirt and coordinated sweater was widely adopted at the beginning of the decade.

Fair Isle patterns

Colorful hand-knit Fair Isle patterns exemplified the characteristic sportswear genre popularized by the Prince of Wales. The simple geometric motifs are essentially stocking stitch produced with more than one color per row.

▼ Sportswear influences

Golf fashions from 1927. The man's V-neck sweater and tie are mirrored by the woman's boyish striped sweater with large collar and tie; both wear polished brogues. Throughout the decade, hemlines rose and the knife-pleat skirt is knee-length.

▶ Knitted bathing suit

A hand-knitted bathing suit modelled in 1926. Although the knitted costume had an unfortunate tendency to sag and become waterlogged when worn, in the absence of elastic fiber only knitted structures provided the necessary fit and ease.

1930s:
The Birth of Knitwear

Knitted garments perfectly exemplified the new silhouette of the 1930s, when, after the brief, body-skimming lines of the 1920s, fit was once again important. The "Bright Young Things" of the previous decade disappeared from view, along with the shimmering short skirts and the wayward ways of the flappers. The fall of the hemline was dramatic and sudden; the January issue of American *Vogue* featured an illustration by Cecil Beaton of a group of women from 1929 wearing above-the-knee skirts, and on the facing page from 1930, the silhouette was seen to change suddenly into "dresses that swept the ground and waists that embraced the middle."

French couturier Jean Patou was the first to lower the hemline. American designers followed suit and Hollywood found itself with a backlog of films made before "the Fall" (*Vogue*'s description of the dramatic drop in hemlines) in which all the heroines were already *démodé*. Not only did the hemlines fall, so, too did the Dow Jones Index. The consequence of the 1929 Wall Street Crash, together with the political uncertainty in Europe, brought a new sobriety to every aspect of cultural life, including fashion. Fortunes disappeared overnight. Harder times were reflected in the long, lean silhouette and youth gave way to a suggestion of womanly curves accentuated by tailoring, which assumed a new importance. Dresses were constructed with innovative seaming and detailing, and the two-piece tailored suit became a wardrobe staple for women. Expensive, luxurious fabrics were replaced by more mundane materials such as corduroy and cotton. Knitted garments were constructed in such a way as to replicate the sturdiness of woven cloth, either through the choice of yarn such as bouclé, or in the stitch structure itself. Lastex, previously confined to swimwear and underwear, began to be used in knitted and woven outwear, providing a neater, tighter fit.

Daywear and the Depression Era

In a society where the gap between the rich and poor grew ever wider, knitwear was available to all. Knitted garments filled the niche in the fashionable wardrobe of the 1930s between Hollywood-inspired glamour and the vogue for tailored daywear that increasing numbers of women wore to work. Manufacturers were quick to respond to the demand for the new leisurewear and moved their production from underwear to outerwear, and the generic term "hosiery" was replaced by "knitwear."

Fashion was in the detail; the simplicity of line allowed for individuality to be expressed through accessories. Costume jewelry, fashionable in the 1920s under the influence of Chanel, assumed an even greater importance; this was the age of the brooch, secured on the lapel of the tailored jacket or shirtdress. Hats moved away from the generic cloche to extravagant designs of tulle-swathed cartwheels, turbans and feathered toques. Elsa Schiaparelli continued to exert a Surrealist influence with her avant-garde approach to accessory design. The straightened circumstances of the Depression era meant that clothes had to be worn for more than one season; accessories were a way of ringing the changes without any major expenditure.

The movie screen provided escapism. Hollywood, experiencing a Golden Age since the stockmarket crash, presented glamourous stars such as Jean Harlow, Carole Lombard and Mae West wearing halterneck silk and satin evening dresses that revealed the line of the body. These were the result of a revolutionary new cutting technique. The bias-cut was invented by Parisian couturier Madeleine Vionnet and utilized by American designer Gilbert Adrian in the 1933 film *Dinner at Eight*. His bias-cut backless dress for Jean Harlow introduced Parisian couture to the mass market, as Hollywood replaced Paris as the arbiter of fashionable style.

Knitwear at this period was mostly concerned with practical daywear. Between 1900 and 1950, women's clothing needs changed dramatically. High fashion in the early twentieth century required the purchase of a custom-made and custom-fitted wardrobe from Parisian couturiers or from American importers and reproducers of Paris models. However, burgeoning educational opportunities for women both in America and Europe opened up careers in teaching, secretarial work and professions that required appropriate clothing. This contributed to the growth of the ready-to-wear industry, whose goal was to make fashionable clothing available to most income levels. American label A&L Tirocchi was established by Italian-born sisters Anna and Laura Tirocchi, who maintained a small, personalized dress business from their home in Providence, Rhode Island, for over 30 years, from 1915 to 1947. Their understanding of the requirements of the modern woman included wool jersey suits, smart for the office, yet relaxed enough for activities in the home, a direct heir of the cardigan suits of Coco Chanel.

BELOW The influence of the Art Deco movement can be seen in the decorative detail deployed in these two dresses. Features such as molded clasps and appliquéd felt flowers were an inexpensive way of updating an outfit. New plastics such as Bakelite were incorporated into garments as novelty clasps or belt buckles. The functional zip fastener became a decorative item once Elsa Schiaparelli featured them in her haute couture designs.

PAGE 46 This crochet-knit dress is evidence of the return to a form-fitting silhouette that replaced the tubular fashions of the previous decade. Designed by Merle Munn and photographed in 1935, it also demonstrates the influence of sports dress on elegant daywear, as seen in the "polo" collar and turnback cuffs.

OPPOSITE A knitted day dress from the Spectator Sports range by American designer and retailer Hattie Carnegie. Following the Wall Street Crash and subsequent Depression, astute entrepreneur and successful retailer Carnegie added to her previously bespoke service a fashionable and affordable ready-to-wear line in 1928, with Norman Norell as the designer. The impact of this garment hinges on a new effect in which the striped sleeves and yoke are knitted as one continual unit. This is attached to the bodice of the dress by a fold in the ground fabric, anchored by a Bakelite bow clasp.

OPPOSITE FAR RIGHT A gold-and-rust striped "cut and sew" stockinette dress features an emerald full-length zip. The knitted belt is given resilience by applied stripes and punctuates the transition from the V-form stripes of the bodice to the horizontal lines of the skirt, which ends high on the calf.

Dressmaking and hand-knitting were necessities that kept poorer families clothed, but it was still possible to follow fashion with the aid of pattern books and the ever-proliferating women's magazines such as *Harper's Bazaar, Vogue, Mademoiselle, Ladies' Home Journal, Woman's Day, McCall's, The New Yorker, Good Housekeeping, Brides, Woman's Home Companion* and *Collier's* magazines. These publications helped women navigate the precarious waters of looking fashionable without spending money and included fashion, etiquette and various craft activities, with accompanying patterns for dresses and sweaters. Although these magazines reflected trends, rather than setting them, they offered an affordable way for women to access fashionable clothing, including knitwear.

The Designed Sweater

The newly revealed womanly curves of the 1930s, with the waist once more in its natural place, were shown to advantage in knitted garments. The construction of geometric ribs and yokes, aided by the flexibility and elasticity intrinsic to the structure of knitted fabrics, emphasized the female form. By increasing or decreasing the number of stitches, garments could be widened or narrowed to accommodate various body shapes without the need for the "fittings" necessary with woven garments.

As the diversification of knitwear from sportswear widened, the simple knitted sweater was now subject to the design process, rather than the engineering skills of the frame-work knitter. Decorative elements crept in, as knitted garments began to be worn for their style rather than their practical qualities. Art Deco remained a strong influence, providing inspiration in terms of color and patterning, or in the buckle of the all-important belt. As in mainstream fashion, there was an obsession with detail and outsized and exaggerated trimmings, particularly novelty buttons in one of the new plastics such as Bakelite. This material was often sculpted into animals, flowers or the geometric patterns of Art Deco. Necklines extended into bows, and the padded shoulders of the era were copied by gathering the sleevehead into the bodice. A rage for anything Egyptian followed the opening of Cecil B. DeMille's 1931 film *Cleopatra*, an epic on the life of Egypt's notorious queen, starring Claudette Colbert. French knots, satin stitch and lazy daisy stitch were all effective in personalizing a hand-knitted dress, together with fringe, pompoms and fur trimmings.

The bolero was popular for both day and evening; a simple jacket shape with a curved center front and short sleeves, ending just above the midriff, the hand-knit version was easy to execute. The use of "lace" frames with mechanized patterning and the Raschel warp-knitting machine provided lighter-weight sweaters that were also suitable for eveningwear, and were often embellished with bugle beads or rhinestone buttons for added effect.

OPPOSITE TOP This four-color striped sweater in mock-rib uses the interplay of mitered and overlaid stripes to evoke the angular geometrics of the Art Deco movement, which is also acknowledged by Bakelite diamond-shape buttons.

OPPOSITE BELOW Neck details, including ruffles, frills or faux scarves, were a feature of tailored daywear. This translates into a buttoned soft jabot below the Peter Pan collar in a sweater by British manufacturer Goodknit.

FAR LEFT Nautical touches were a recurring theme during this era of ocean-going travel and sailing. This short-sleeved sweater from 1935, designed by Schiaparelli, has a knotted and attached cravat in two-color peppercorn tuck stitch. The same stitch decorates the sleeves.

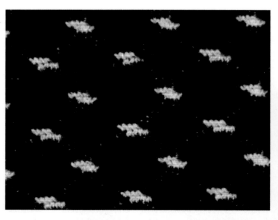

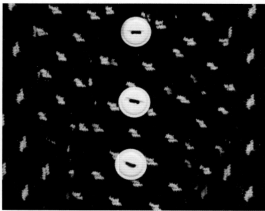

ABOVE AND LEFT Details of the Goodknit sweater: the manufacturer's label, a close-up of the all-over knit, and the three-button jabot. The "powdered" two-color pattern is attained by the use of warp inlaid yarns in cream, inserted by means of wrap or lace bars.

RIGHT AND DETAIL BELOW
The gold, marigold, primrose and brown chevron pattern of this rayon sweater is achieved by distorting stripes in crochet; easy matching across the sleeve head is allowed by continuing the stripe down to the hem of the short sleeve.

BELOW Artist Sonia Delaunay's experiments with blocks of color influenced the design of this hand-knitted sweater dating from 1935. The graphic effect arises simply from patching together rectangular panels of double moss stitch in contrasting colors.

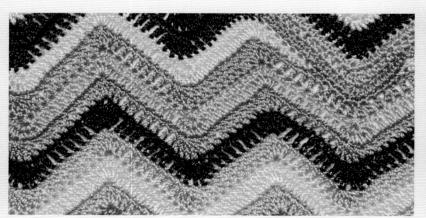

LEFT AND BELOW In this Shetland wool, hand-knit sweater, the chevron stripe arises from the distortions in "wale-deflection" lace, sometimes called "feather and fan" stitch in knitting circles. Short sleeves, held closed by a 2X1 rib and raised high by the fullness of the sleeve head, give the shoulder emphasis, which is reinforced by the zip detail and square neckline.

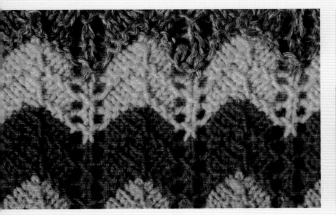

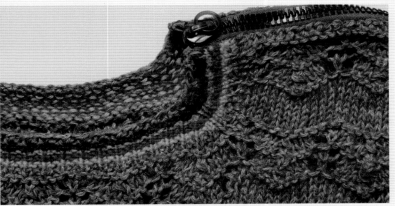

Pringle of Scotland

The manufacturing company most closely associated with traditional knitwear is Pringle of Scotland. Founded by Robert Pringle in 1815 in the rich sheep-raising area of the Scottish Borders, the company claims to be the first to use cashmere in knitted outerwear in 1930, the first British manufacturer to understand the value of employing a designer and to be the inventor of the iconic twinset.

Between the world wars the international knitwear industry developed rapidly, particularly in Italy, but it was the Scottish who were renowned for the best quality, if not the most fashionable knitwear. At this time production at Pringle still included hosiery as well as outerwear. In 1927 the company began to manufacture pure silk stockings, called Prinseta, which in 1931 were successfully relaunched as Rodono Splashproof, the tartan packaging bearing the portraits of the five queens of Europe and the claim that "they never wore any other stockings."

The European manufacturers understood knitwear was subject to the same demands for fashionability as woven outerwear, a concept that moved Pringle to employ a designer, Otto Weisz. The son of a Viennese surgeon, he served his apprenticeship with knitting manufacturers Bernhard Altmann of Vienna before moving to Scotland. By 1934 Pringle was able to pioneer the first collection of Scottish sweaters to feature design details such as collars, cuffs, peplums, and plackets, all aimed at the American market. Hugh Barty-King's book *Pringle of Scotland* includes this description from the company's 1937 spring catalogue:

> *Pringle Sportswear is designed for the woman of refined taste – for the woman who demands to be comfortably and faultlessly clad for an inexpensive outlay. The exclusive models shown in this booklet are made in purest Indian cashmere and finest Botany yarn; they are distinctively endowed with that subtle charm and inherent quality of good taste which has made them famous in the salons of London, Paris and New York. You may choose with confidence from this select assembly – for 'occasions' or for every day, they are reassuringly RIGHT.*

At the time, the cost of a Pringle sweater would provide a week's food for a family of four. Such an expensive garment was aimed at the "landed gentry," as a brochure from Adderly's of Leicester claims:

> *The 'landed gentry' are never more distinguished than when they are in sports clothes – and why? Simply because their sweaters and tweeds are of the highest class Scotch make, with the breath of the moors and outdoor life about them.*

ABOVE A close-fitting hand-knit golf sweater with "grown-on" wide round-neck rib and integral breast pocket. Styled with hat by Rose Descat and gloves by Hermès, photographed in 1933 by George Hoyningen-Huene.

RIGHT Classic Argyle-patterned intarsia fabric. It's normal for the evolution of the diamonds and diagonals to be based on a two-in-one gradient since this produces a slightly elongated form, which appears more elegant.

OPPOSITE This waist-length skating sweater dating from 1936 is hand-knitted in graduated horizontal stripes over which are diagonal lines of fancy slip and purl stitch following the diagonal button fastening on the back.

Scottish knitwear companies capitalized on the fact that the British royal family spent their summers at Balmoral, the much-loved home of Queen Victoria, just as Scotland's globally renowned golf courses, a game that originated in Scotland, added to the appeal of Pringle's golfing sweaters.

Innovative developments by the company included the patenting of Slimfit underwear in 1932. Rubber or Lastex was added to silk, wool or cotton to produce a "reduced waist garment," which slimmed down the body beneath the bias-cut evening dresses of the period. Rodono Slimfit vests, knickers and combinations were all available with low-cut backs to accommodate this trend. The company is also credited with the creation of the intarsia design known as the Argyle pattern, incorporated into golfing sweaters, a tradition that continues to this day. In 1955 Pringle formalized their relationship with golf by producing the Ryder Cup golf shirt, a closely textured garment knitted on a fine-gauge machine also used for men's underwear. This marked the introduction of men's knitted outerwear to their brand.

BELOW A 1930s hand-knitted child's twinset incorporates the popular Fair Isle patterning in Shetland wool.

OPPOSITE Fifteen miles north of the English–Scottish border lies the town of Hawick. One of Britain's richest sheep-farming regions, it was a natural progression for the area to become the site of those knitwear manufacturers keen to capitalize on this local natural resource. Since the seventeenth century, the Borders knitwear industry has thrived and includes world-renowned brand names such as Hogg of Hawick, Ballantyne, Dalkeith, Pringle and Braemar, of which the illustration is an example.

THE TWINSET

The classic British twinset was not initially "designed" but engineered. Categorized as sportswear, it combined a cardigan buttoned up to the neck with a short-sleeved round-necked sweater. A classic garment, when worn with a string of pearls and a tweed skirt, it came to represent a way of life, one that upheld middle-class values and also represented restrained good taste. Beloved of style icons such as Grace Kelly, the twinset has sustained its popularity from the 1930s to the present day. Although the twinset developed variations over the following decades, with minor adjustments to the shape of the neckline and length of sleeves, and occasionally the inclusion of pattern and decoration, the basic premise remained the same; the two garments are invariably constructed in the same color, yarn and stitch.

SPORTSWEAR & UNDERWEAR

D4753 JUMPER · D4754 CARDIGAN

A Twin=set in pure Cashmere with the Cardi=
gan in this instance in the always becoming
short style. Note the two useful pockets.
In a large range of colours.

Price: JUMPER 37/6 CARDIGAN 47/6

*We will gladly send you a
copy of our new "Braemar"
Booklet with illustrations of
different styles, together with
the name and address of your
nearest retailer.*

OBTAINABLE FROM ALL LEADING STORES

Wholesale from Innes, Henderson & Co. Ltd., of Hawick, Scotland
and at Axtell House, Warwick Street, London, W.1

Sports for All

Something new has appeared. It could be called a movement, a wave, a passion, a new feeling for life; this is a reality that has inundated, pursued, inspired, reformed and influenced millions of people. … Body culture, gymnastics, dance … the entire Western world and its sphere of influence has been transformed by this strange new sensibility and way of life.

Wolfgang Graeser,
Body Sense: Gymnastics, Dance, Sport, 1927

The increasing preoccupation with sports during the 1920s accelerated to become an international obsession in the following decade. Sports became integral to every way of life, from the upper-class passion for skiing to the Women's League of Health and Beauty in Great Britain, which popularized physical fitness. Founded in 1930 their motto was "Movement is Life," and the regime of keep-fit exercise and callisthenics was accessible to everyone. Certain sports, however, were the remit of only the rich and leisured: weekends in the country, skiing and shooting in winter and tennis parties in the summer.

The knitted bathing suit played its part in pushing boundaries of what was considered immodest or inappropriate for these activities. Worn for sunbathing, swimming and diving, the bathing suit allowed photographers of the day such as George Hoyningen-Heuene to disseminate images of near nudity that paved the way for more liberating clothes in other areas of sport; in 1931 tennis player Mrs. Fearnley-Whitingstall appeared on court stockingless, while golfing sweaters for women were allowed to be sleeveless. Tennis dresses had plunging backs to the new waistline, a look that was to extend to the Hollywood stars in their backless eveningwear.

During this period, the majority of knitwear was still categorized as sportswear. The properties of knitted fabric rendered it uniquely suitable for outdoor activities. Fibers in woollen yarn capture the air, providing warmth without weight and allowing the skin to breathe. The flexibility of the fabric allowed for freedom of movement, whether it be for the swing of the golf club or the practicality of pliable knitted jersey for the exertions of tennis. René Lacoste, winner of the Tennis Open championship in 1926, went on to establish his clothing company with the knitwear manufacturer André Gillier in 1933, providing future decades with a design classic.

OPPOSITE By the 1930s the Jaegar brand represented fashionable sportswear, as can be seen in this skiing outfit. The collar and faux button band are fashioned in rib jacquard in three colors whereas the body panels, sleeves and hat are ladder-back jacquard, omitting three out of four needles on the reverse.

ABOVE A 1933 illustration by Anna Zinkeisen shows an array of knitwear: from left, Robert Douglas, Jaeger, Henri & Mawdsley, Leathercraft and Fortnum & Mason.

Regional Knits of the British Isles

Sports were emphasized for their health-giving aspects, and the period saw the advent of social clubs devoted to such community sports as mass bicycle rides. In England the working classes were urged by the government to spend their weekends hiking in the countryside and "rambling" clubs formed, requiring practical clothing, of which a Guernsey, Jersey or Aran sweater was an integral item of clothing for both men and women.

Rugged, dark-colored woollen Guernseys were a staple of fishermen's gear all over the British Isles. They were constructed from oiled wool to render them waterproof and featured patterns and stitch structures indigenous to a specific area. Increasingly worn for the more demanding outdoor activities such as hiking, the fisherman's sweater was adapted by regional knitters to suit the contemporary market by substituting softer, unoiled undyed yarns.

Channel Islands

Records of knitted goods bought from the Channel Islands, off the west coast of France, date back to Elizabethan times. The cottage industry for making woollen stockings and waistcoats on Guernsey and Jersey thrived throughout most of the seventeenth and eighteenth centuries. The Guernsey sweater came into being as a garment for seamen, who required a warm, durable yet comfortable item of clothing that would resist the sea spray. The hard twist given to the tightly packed wool fibers in the spinning process and the tightly knitted stitches produced a finish that would "turn water" and render the sweater almost waterproof.

Most coastal communities in the British Isles had a "gansey," which derived from the original Guernsey. In those days Guernseys had the distinctive patterns of each parish to which the wearer belonged, so that it was possible to identify an unlucky sailor by his knitwear, should he meet a watery end. These square-shaped garments, made out of thick wool, were often knitted in the round on sets of four or five needles. Fishermen's sweaters became popular as leisurewear in the 1880s and a fashionable version was even worn by women. Coco Chanel incorporated a fisherman's sweater into her French Riviera chic, wearing hers with faux jewelry and a scarf tied as a belt.

There are several characteristics of sweaters from the Channel Islands, including a decorative knotted edge created by the knotted cast-on stitch. The rib at the top of the sleeve is said to represent a sailing ship's rope ladder in the rigging; the raised seam across the shoulder, a rope; and the garter-stitch panel, waves breaking upon the beach. The gussets under the arm and at the neck are for ease of movement, as are the splits at the hem. The body usually consists of a plain stocking stitch.

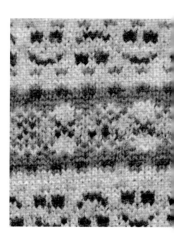

ABOVE AND BELOW Fair Isle patterning was a natural choice for children's sweaters, particularly when rendered in a brighter color palette rather than the more traditional browns and beige.

OPPOSITE Located among cherry blossom and daffodils, this single jersey two-piece suit is destined for springtime wear. The illustration for J & J McCallum appeared in a women's magazine.

LOOK FOR THIS LABEL ON KNITWEAR—IT IS A GUARANTEE OF COLOUR, QUALITY AND STYLE.

J & J McCALLUM LTD PAISLEY SCOTLAND

McCALLUM DYED
BRITISH C.A.W.D.A.

Aran Islands

The Aran Islands are located off the west of Ireland, in Galway Bay. The typical cable-patterned Aran sweater is a nineteenth-century invention, prompted by the government-appointed Congested Districts Board in 1891 to help poor families survive unemployment by encouraging local people to knit garments commercially. The craftspeople exploited their indigenous craft by linking the patterns of the knitwear to ancient myths and cultures, resulting in some styles of regional knitting dating no further back than the start of the twentieth century. It was during this period that knitted Aran sweaters were sold to tourists from shops in cities such as Dublin and they soon became known worldwide.

By the twentieth century this cottage industry began to thrive, and the Board trained knitters to create complex patterns from stitches such as honeycomb, figure eight and double diamond. *Vogue Knitting* published an Aran pattern in 1956 and the design became popular in America. Aran knitting can be simulated by machine processes, but hand-knitted sweaters are still much sought after.

Shetland Islands

The Shetlands is a group of islands north of the Scottish mainland, and initially the hand-knitters there produced quantities of coarse woollen stockings and blankets. Frame-made hosiery could produce these more cheaply, and a hand-knitted alternative was required. In 1830 the Shetland islanders began making lace shawls, which were an immediate commercial success. The same lace technique was applied to other products including spencers (women's bodices, then worn as underwear) and from the 1920s onwards, pullover sweaters and cardigans. Unst, the most northerly island, produced a very finely spun yarn that was ideal for making lace shawls and scarves, being exceptionally soft and warm. The wool was taken from the throat of the indigenous sheep by plucking rather than clipping.

Improved transport links between the islands and mainland attracted visitors to the Shetlands. Aware of the local knitting skills, they brought fashionable lace articles to be copied. The intricate openwork stitches, invented by the islanders, were given picturesque names such as "fern," "horseshoe" and "catspaw," and the paisley "cone" was popular.

In Shetlands lace-knitting, the articles have no cast-on or cast-off edge, but start from a single stitch, with edges knitted on the bias. The web-like patterns are worked back and forth on two flexible metal needles on a ground of garter stitch. A typical shawl would have an elaborately patterned middle, framed with a deep inner border, and finished with a vandyked (pointed) edging. Contemporary retailers still pass the shawls through a wedding ring to show off their fineness and flexibility.

LEFT An example of Aran knitting in ecru wool: the stock references of moss stitch, four-needle cable, open tuck and banded, wale, deflected diamonds are all featured.

BELOW Combining practicality with femininity, and redolent of the boudoir, this luxurious knitted dressing gown in powder blue Shetland wool lace is edged in swansdown.

THIS PAGE The simple understated classic twinset has evolved here into a decorative outfit of matching sweater and cardigan. Hand-knitted in two-ply yarn, it employs a repertoire of stitches, including eyelet lace, garter stitch and small cables overlaid by contrast sprigs of simple embroidery and French knots.

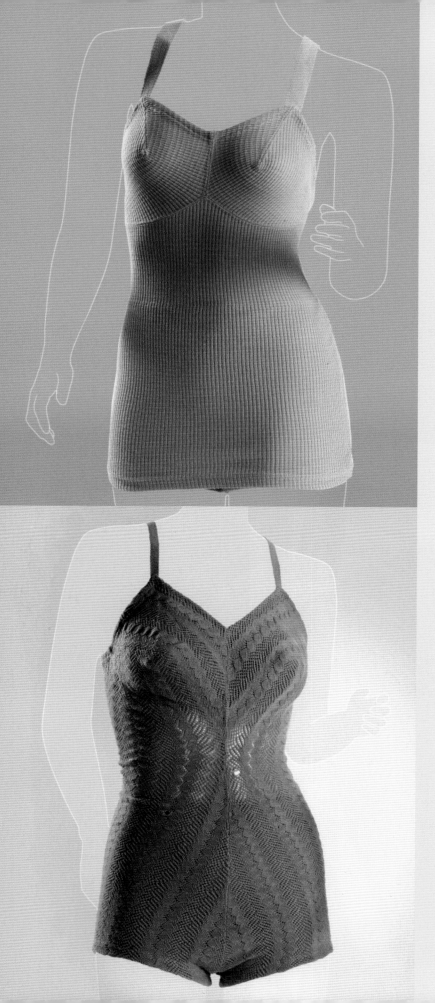

Swimwear Pioneers

The cult of health and sports was an increasing preoccupation in both America and Europe during the early decades of the twentieth century. When Australian swim star Annette Kellerman introduced a simple one-piece wool-knitted style to the U.S. during her 1907 tour (and was subsequently arrested for indecent exposure), wool knitted suits soon began to be manufactured. Given that the structure of knitted fabric allowed for ease of movement and yet clung to the body, the segue from hosiery and underwear to bathing suits was both direct and inevitable for knitwear manufacturers. The trio of great American swimwear companies, Jantzen, Catalina and Cole, all had their provenance in the knitwear industry. American manufacturers, rather than their European counterparts, were quick to exploit the market for machine-knitted bathing suits, eventually diversifying into active sportswear and creating a flourishing West Coast fashion industry. The skill of Catalina, Jantzen and Cole was to harness the interest in physical fitness to fashion trends and to associate their products with the glamour of Hollywood stars and starlets, always eager for the pin-up photo opportunity. Ginger Rogers, Joan Crawford, Ronald Reagan and Marilyn Monroe were all photographed in Catalina sportswear for advertising and publicity purposes.

Jantzen produced their first commercial bathing suit in 1915. The innovative suit allowed bathers to discard the cumbersome gathers and folds of the Edwardian era for a suit comprising long shorts attached to a sleeveless clinging skirted top, which came in vibrant colors with stripes. Initially known as the Portland Knitting Company, and founded in 1910 by Roy and John A Zehntbauer and Carl Jantzen in Portland, Oregon, the company owned a few knitting machines above a small retail store, producing hosiery and sweaters. The partners developed their first bathing suit through their affiliation to the Portland rowing club, developing a pair of swimming trunks, which replaced the bulky traditional drawstring shorts with a ribbed body knitted on machines that normally produced sweater cuffs (ribbers). The company refined the structure by using a finer-gauge needle on specially adapted knitting machines to produce the first one-piece in a ribbed stitch.

In 1918 the name was changed to Jantzen Knitting Mills and in 1940 the company became Jantzen Inc. Jantzen is recognized by the insignia of the Diving Girl, one of the oldest of fashion brand icons and which first appeared in advertisements for the company in the 1920s. Designed by Frank and Florenz Clark, the logo was embroidered or sewn onto Jantzen swimsuits from 1923, at the same time as the tag-line "The Suit that Changed Bathing to Swimming" appeared. In 1938 Jantzen established separate men's and women's

OPPOSITE TOP The straight edge at the hem of the 1930s bathing suit by John Smedley conceals the attached shorts beneath. A shaped bodice has intermittent rows of inlaid thread to maintain the form of the basic wool fabric.

OPPOSITE BELOW This transfer lace wool bathing suit by John Smedley, also from the 1930s, is lined to form an integral bra top and briefs. The distorted vertical stripe in the lace adds to the suggestion of a curvaceous form at the waist.

RIGHT The introduction of Lastex, an elasticated yarn, in addition to the woollen fiber is responsible for the firm texture and flexible structure of this bathing costume. Additionally, the vertical stripe indicates that the knit is rotated, producing a fabric with enhanced lateral recovery.

divisions, going on to win six Woolknit awards for men's sweater designs between 1965 and 1980. However, in 1997, the sportswear lines were discontinued and today the company concentrates solely on swimwear.

Catalina Sportswear evolved from a small California knitting mill manufacturing underwear and sweaters into a swimwear brand leader. Founded in 1907 by John C. Bentz as Bentz Knitting Mills, the company was renamed Pacific Knitting Mills in 1912, Catalina Knitting Mills in 1928 and Catalina from 1955, subsequently combining with Cole of California to become Catalina Cole. Catalina produced increasingly daring and fashion-led swimwear throughout the 1920s, particularly the boldly striped Chicken suit, the men's Speed suit and ribstitch S. suits before expanding its lines to include knitwear and sportswear. Frank Smith, who went on to head Evan Picone for Saks Fifth Avenue, designed womenswear, while John Norman created the menswear lines.

Cole of California was founded by Fred Cole, a former actor at Universal Studios whose family owned the underwear manufacturers, West Coast Knitting Mills. Finding underwear design uninspiring, Cole turned his talents to swimwear. His first swimsuit design was the provocative Prohibition suit. Commercially successful, it became known as the first true fashion swimsuit. Film costumer Margit Fellegi, employed by Cole in 1932, immediately utilized the rubberized and stretch possibilities of new fibers that could surpass the old wool knits, combining technology with a design ability honed by her work in Hollywood.

By the mid 1930s knitted wool swimsuits were eased into history. California designer Mabs of Hollywood began to fashion swimwear from Lastex, a woven satin-finish elastic and silk material developed by the United States Rubber Company, first used for girdle manufacture. Beryl Williams writes in *Fashion Is Our Business*, in 1948:

> Bathing suit manufacturers had not been unaware of the advantages of Lastex at that time, but they had not been too successful at knitting the elastic yarn into suits after the style of the wool knit suits of the period. Mr. and Mrs. Barnes (Mabs and Voris), *on the other hand, who had had Lastex woven for their garments, had an idea one day. Why not bathing suits of woven Lastex, too?*

Initially rejected by manufacturers who deemed the suits too daring, and too much like a foundation garment, Mabs designed and manufactured a gold-colored suit for Jean Harlow, prompting screen siren Marlene Dietrich to visit Bullocks department store to order a dozen in every color. The day of the knitted bathing suit came to an abrupt end, causing leading swimwear manufacturers to deploy the new woven technology, and also to diversify into knitted and woven active sportswear.

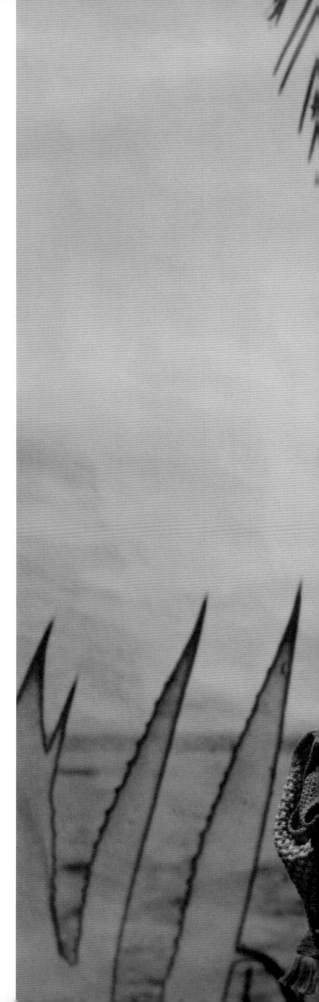

NOBLE FIBERS

Noble fiber is the term used for the rarest, most expensive and luxurious of yarns. The reason for their rarity may lie with the geographical inaccessibility of the yarn's source, the relative scarcity of the breed, which might require certain climate conditions to survive, and also in the political complexities of the indigenous country.

Alpaca: *Vicugna pacos* is a domesticated species of the South American camelid. It resembles a small llama in appearance. Alpacas are kept in herds that graze on the level heights of the Andes of Ecuador, southern Peru, Northern Bolivia and northern Chile at an altitude of 11,483 ft (3,500 m) to 16,404 ft (5000 m) above sea level, throughout the year. They are bred specifically for their fiber, and have been domesticated for thousands of years. Alpaca comes in a wide variety of natural colors – Peru classifies 52, Australia 12 and the United States 16, reducing the need for toxic dyes that harm the environment. In the textile industry, "alpaca" primarily refers to the hair of Peruvian alpacas, but more broadly it refers to a style of fabric originally made from alpaca hair but now often made from similar fibers, such as mohair and Icelandic sheep wool.

Alpaca fleece is lustrous and silky, and unlike sheep's wool, it bears no lanolin, making it hypoallergenic. The preparing, carding, spinning and finishing process of alpaca is very similar to the process used for wool.

Angora: The extremely soft hair of the angora rabbit. The hair of the angora goat is referred to as "mohair." These soft, seductive fibers were the favorite of the 1940s "Sweater Girls."

LEFT The darted sleeve head, providing a square shoulder, and the high-buttoning neckline of this semi-tailored cashmere cardigan were an indication of the more masculine silhouette that was to come in the 1940s. Photographed in 1938 by Toni Frissell.

Camel hair: The two-humped Bactrian camel from Outer Mongolia has a soft under-layer of hair which is warm yet light. The hair is usually left undyed, as it is naturally a pleasing pale toffee-brown color. In the 1950s the fibers were popular for twinsets.

Cashmere: A luxurious "noble" fiber, originally hair from the downy undercoat of the Asiatic goat (*Capra hircus laniger*) with a diameter of many hundredths of an inch. Similar hair from animals bred selectively from the feral goat populations of Australia, New Zealand and Scotland is regarded as cashmere, provided the fiber diameter is similar. The finest cashmere, however, is from China, originating in a small district to the west of Beijing and another in Manchuria.

Before the First World War the purest fleeces came from the remote southern frontiers of Imperial Russia, the mountains of the Caucasus and Turkestan. As with most animals living in a cold climate, the "cashmere goat" is provided with long, coarse outer hairs and a warm undercoat of fine fleece with excellent non-conducting properties – ounce for ounce, it has three times the insulation value of lamb's wool. It gives warmth without weight and is distinctive in its luster; it does not have the elastic, resilient quality of wool from a sheep, but does have perfect draping qualities.

The expense lies in the small amount of fleece obtained from each goat: a male produces 4 oz (125 g), a female 2 oz (50 g) a year. A year's yield from four to six animals is needed to make a sweater. It is never shorn with shears, but plucked by hand from the underbellies of the gats. The finest cashmere is found on animals living in the heights of the mountain ranges. From its source the fleeces are carried by yaks, camels and horses to the port of Tien-tsin on a journey that may take the best part of a year. From there the raw fiber is shipped to a processor who dyes it, then sells it on to a spinner, who sells it to a knitwear manufacturer as a spun yarn.

Sea Island cotton: An exceptionally fine, long, staple type of cotton *Gossypium barbadense*, grown formerly in Sea Island, off the coast of Georgia.

Silk: Silk is a natural protein fiber. The best-known type is obtained from cocoons made by the larvae of the mulberry silkworm *Bombyx mori* reared in captivity (sericulture). Silk's unique luster occurs because the filament is the finest of all natural fibers. Despite its delicacy, it is extremely strong.

Vicuña: The vicuña (*Vicugna vicugna*) is one of two wild South American camelids along with the guanoco, which live in the high alpine areas of the Andes, at an altitude of 18,000 ft (5,500 m) where only nutrient-poor, tough bunch grasses and festuca grow. The animals are most commonly found in Bolivia, Peru, Chile, southwest Colombia, central Ecuador and northwest Argentina. The vicuña is a relative of the llama and is now believed to be the wild ancestor of domesticated alpacas. Vicuñas produce small amounts of extremely fine wool, which is very expensive because the animal can only be shorn every three years. The thick but soft coat is a special adaptation that traps layers of warm air close to its body so it can tolerate the freezing temperatures. Its warming properties come from the tiny scales on the hollow air-filled fibers, which cause the fibers to interlock and trap insulating air. The vicuña yields the finest, softest and costliest natural fiber in the world, substantially finer, softer and lighter than the very best cashmere or angora. The fleece is sensitive to chemical treatment, so the wool is usually left in its natural color.

The Incas considered the vicuña a sacred animal. Once every four years the king would order a *chaccu*, the rounding up of vicuña to be sheared and then released unharmed. Only royalty was allowed to wear the golden fleece. The tradition continues today with Andean communities carrying out the *chaccu* annually under the strict guidelines of Convention on International Trade in Endangered Species (CITES) welfare and preservation.

Ironically the bounty of the animal's fleece – which so very nearly led to its extinction in the 1960s (when only 6,000 animals were left) – is now contributing to ensure its survival and that of the native communities in the Andean mountains. The trade in vicuña fiber is strictly licensed and every product accompanied by a certificate and approved by CITES.

Other natural yarns

Cotton: The seed hair of a wide variety of plants of the Gossypium family.

Linen: Describes yarns spun exclusively from flax fibers.

Shetland yarn: A fiber spun by hand in the Shetland Islands from the sheep bred and reared in those islands.

▲ Golf sweaters
During the 1930s the boundaries between sportswear and outerwear began to disappear, achieving a relaxed, yet sophisticated elegance in both areas. Photographed in 1932, Daphne de Levis Prizer wears a knitted golf blouse that offers freedom of movement with chic styling.

Key looks of the decade
1930s

▶ Art Deco patterns
Art Deco continued to influence the patterning on knitwear design. Austrian in origin, this "Swiss-darned" hand-knit alpaca sweater features a geometric key pattern and dates from 1935.

▶ Metallics
Embroidery and knits using metallic threads were an important fashion look among Hollywood's younger players. Here Kitty Carlisle, in Paramount's *She Loves Me Not* in 1934, endorses a sports frock in a royal blue knit with silver for afternoon wear.

Hollywood influences
Costumers for the American motion-picture industry, such as Adrian, Travis Banton and William Plunkett, brought movie-star style to the masses. Movie costumes were also featured in such fashion magazines as *Women's Wear Daily* and *Vogue*.

◀ Jersey playclothes

Playclothes were introduced in the 1930s, and knitted jersey provided an inexpensive, easy-care and comfortable outfit for recreation. Here two women are wearing jersey "sylo-jamas" in red, white and blue while skating on the roof of the Roosevelt Hotel in New York, 1933.

▶ Lean silhouettes

An illustration from *Vogue* dating from 1934 shows three knitted ensembles. The waistline is now back in its natural place, the length once more mid-calf, and details such as the pussy-cat bow around the neck, the Bakelite buttons and the laced fastening of the cardigan (right) were important new achievements.

Boleros and short jackets

Tailored boleros and capelets, often richly embellished, were worn over the bias-cut gowns of the 1930s. The bolero jacket became a signature Schiaparelli design. The shrug is a less structured version.

Plastic zips

The metal zip had been invented in 1893 but didn't become widely used until the 1930s. Schiaparelli was one of the first couturiers to use plastic colored zips. For London fashions she used zips from the British Lightening Fastener Company, while in Paris she used those made by Éclair, and for export to America, the Hookless Fastener Company.

1940s:
Knitting for All

The onset of the Second World War introduced a previously unknown level of democratization into fashion. Notions of class-based and elitist styles were overturned as civilians and the armed services dressed alike. Tailored suits, designed in Britain by Queen Elizabeth's couturier Norman Hartnell and in America, designer to the stars Gilbert Adrian, provided a couture cut and uniform for all.

The French haute couture industry ceased to be a force for change, as the designers dispersed or closed down their houses. In 1939 Schiaparelli moved to New York, Vionnet retired and Chanel ceased trading following the occupation of Paris. Europe's loss was America's gain; in 1940 Charles James and Mainbocher opened their first New York couture houses. The silhouette, which had shown every indication of returning to the hourglass figure with the introduction of the corset by Mainbocher in 1940, now reverted to practicality and austerity as conscription meant that the majority of the younger population was wearing a uniform. Isolation from the influence of European couturiers gave momentum to the American designers who were already eager to define a uniquely American style. Norman Norell, Clare Potter and Claire McCardell produced ready-to-wear fashion based on mix-and-match separates and layered dressing that represented the best of American sportswear.

The Depression of the 1930s had resulted in a slump in output of the spinning, weaving and knitting manufacturers of the industrial Midlands and the Scottish Borders in Great Britain. With the onset of war and government contracts, these underwent a revival, ensuring that although the majority of their output clothed the armed services, knitted products for the civilian population were also available. Knitted structures provided the most practical element of wartime dressing. Easy to launder, warm without being heavy or restrictive, and ultimately recyclable, the majority of knitwear was hand-knitted and often decorated in individual, idiosyncratic style.

With the liberation of Paris in 1944, French haute couture reasserted itself. Christian Dior set up his own house with the backing of Marcel Boussac, and launched his New Look in 1947, elevating fashion once again to an elite art form.

Wartime Restrictions and Utility Clothing

Improvisation and ingenuity were required to fulfill the requirements of everyday wartime life during the 1940s. Clothes were no exception, particularly after rationing commenced in Britain in 1941. The Board of Trade had rules and regulations on hem lengths, coupons and the Utility Clothing Scheme – a set of approved garments designed by several prominent names including Hardy Amies and Norman Hartnell, the Queen's own dressmaker. These official Utility clothes were always distinguished by the CC41 label and, like the designer collaborations with the high street today, these cheap, democratic garments gave women, who could never normally afford haute couture, a chance to experience the cut of well-designed garments.

Wool and cotton were in short supply; the sea shipping routes that were used to import goods were too dangerous, and yet not enough of a priority for government protection. Silk was needed to make parachutes and there was a ban on its use for both clothing and hosiery, one of the reasons women started to wear slacks and trousers. Wool was blended with less-scarce fibers or recycled.

The fashion silhouette reflected the fact that conscription resulted in many women working outside the home for the first time. There was an inevitable relationship between the female uniform of the services and the fashion on "civvy" street. Straight skirts fell to just below the knee, fitted jackets had sharp, padded shoulders, and trimmings were eradicated from collars and pockets – these tweed suits had to last. Subdued colors were of a uniform drabness: air-force blue, khaki, brown and black; manmade dyes were available only in limited quantities since they were created from the same base chemicals needed in dynamite manufacture.

In the United States restrictions were less severe. Although the government order L85 issued in 1943 regulated various aspects of clothing manufacture, these were not as stringent nor as rigidly adhered to as in Britain, being directed at the manufacturers in an attempt to freeze the silhouette and discourage any temptation to innovate trends. Hollywood costumer Gilbert Adrian influenced the design of the Victory suit, the American version of Britain's Utility suit. The screen siren of 1930s Hollywood had been replaced by a new version of womanhood, one who coped admirably with the struggles of wartime life, while wearing fashion that reflected her competence and drive: Adrian clothed her in structured suits with innovative tailoring and exemplary fit.

Hand-knitting underwent an understandable re-surgence during the war years, its practice being perceived almost as a public duty, and was necessarily utilitarian. British yarn supplier Sirdar Wools commanded, "if you can knit, you can do your bit." Knitting for the armed services required some method of quality control so that homemade offerings attained a uniform standard. In the U.K. the Personal Service League acted as agent for the Wool Control Board to ensure a consistent quality of yarn.

PAGE 72 Photographed in 1947 by Horst P Horst, this daywear dress utilizes all the qualities of fine wool jersey, from the draping of the skirt to the molding of the form-fitting bodice. It features lightly padded shoulders and oversize buttons.

ABOVE Utility clothing was labelled with the CC41 mark, Civilian Clothing 1941. The pattern on this Argyle pullover is produced in striped-back three-color jacquard on a circular garment-length machine to avoid the expense of sewing side seams.

OPPOSITE TOP John Smedley began to develop "cut and sew" garments, applying the same pattern-making and manufacturing techniques to knitted cloth as to woven materials. Here a tailored double-jersey mock rib jacket features wide reveres and a darted sleeve head.

OPPOSITE BELOW Outerwear in double jersey was a sturdy replacement for jackets and coats of woven cloth, difficult to source in wartime. This jacket, also by John Smedley, is cut along military lines, with metal-buttoned patch pockets and a high neckline.

"Make Do and Mend" – The British Experience

Knitwear was more vital than ever since fuel was rationed and heating in houses was limited. The famous phrase "make do and mend" was never more aptly applied than to knitwear, since small lengths of wool could be gathered and recycled to create new garments, a necessary ploy since knitwear was included in the restrictions on the amount of clothing that could be purchased under the 1941 Utility scheme. This allowed a yearly ration of 66 coupons per person. One coupon was worth just 2 oz (50 g) of wool. A further 24 oz (600 g) of free wool was supplied for those wishing to knit for the forces, but a year later this was restricted to recognized "knitting parties."

To supplement this government-sanctioned austerity, home dressmaking and knitting came into their own. Not only sweaters were knitted; hardwearing stitches such as twisted ribs and moss stitch were used to create garments that could compete with the warmth and durability of woven-cloth jackets and coats. Cardigans were buttoned up to the neck for maximum warmth and finished on the waist, so that they could be worn under a uniform jacket. Fashionable trends were still adhered to, and the padded shoulders of the tailored suit were replicated in sweaters by the construction of the shoulderpad, knitted in stocking stitch and then folded in half with two layers of cotton wool inserted.

The *Make Do and Mend* pamphlet of 1943 encouraged and advised women on how to make the best of their existing clothes. Knitters employed ingenious techniques to make the wool go further, including combining the yarn from several unraveled garments into one. (The skeins of unraveled yarn were put into the top of a steamer for ten minutes to get out the kinks and then hung up to dry.) The resulting mix of random colors was successfully transformed into Fair Isle designs or similar patterns to make shortwaisted cardigans or V-neck sleeveless waistcoats for either sex. Openwork lacy patterns, such as the feather, leaf, lattice, chevron and shell stitch, stretched the yarn even further and provided garments with an element of much-needed glamour for evening occasions, particularly with the inclusion of beads, pearls and sequins.

There were no government restrictions on the use of trimmings and design details as there were on outwear, which gave the knitter ample opportunity to innovate and decorate sweaters and cardigans with appliqué, knitted corsages, beading and embroidery. Ingenuity came into play when shortages occurred; buttons were crocheted circles stuffed with cotton wool. Knitters were advised to knit up the back and the front of the garment at the same time in case the wool ran out and the yoke and shoulders could be finished in a different yarn.

LEFT Knitting patterns proliferated during the 1940s. Although austerity was a prerequisite for everyday life, the desire for adornment nevertheless triumphed, as evidenced by this complex and colorful design for a hand-knitted sweater featuring a multicolored Aran-style blister stitch on the yoke.

BELOW Lace stitches and openwork structures made yarn go further, as in this pattern for a hand-knit ribbed sweater. The openwork yoke also provided a decorative design feature.

THIS PAGE A handcrafted cardigan epitomizes the "make do and mend" ethos of the period. Ingenious solutions to make the most of odds and ends of yarn included such devices as these crocheted flowers appliquéd to a mesh background, giving the same effect as guipure lace, and completed with fancy purl hand-knit sleeves and trimmings.

Knitting for Victory in the U.S.: *Purl Harder*

The president's wife, Eleanor Roosevelt, was a high-profile proponent of the idea of "knitting for victory." She was frequently photographed at work on another pair of socks or a sweater. Just before Pearl Harbor – with the war already raging in Europe – *Life* magazine ran a cover story on "How to Knit" with the advice: "To the great American question 'What can I do to help the war effort?' the commonest answer yet found is 'Knit.'" Knitting was also part of the government campaign, Bundles for Britain, initiated in order to help both the American soldiers abroad and to provide relief for the beleaguered British people. The bombing of Pearl Harbor and America's entrance into war increased popular efforts to produce more garments. As *Time* magazine reported on July 21, 1940, "The men hardly have time to grab their guns before their wives and sweethearts grab their needles and yarn." The American Red Cross provided standard patterns for all useful garments, which were then exchanged within communities of knitters. Productivity was increased with each individual knitter producing the same garment. Women were encouraged to produce more socks than anything else. This need is aptly demonstrated by the fact that American POWs often unraveled their sweaters and re-knitted themselves socks using straightened barbed wire as needles.

Hollywood stars were co-opted to the cause, with publicity shots of such leading ladies as Rita Hayworth photographed on set with knitting needles in hand.

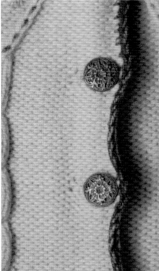

ABOVE The First Lady, Mrs. Franklin D. Roosevelt, is photographed knitting by Thomas D. Mcavoy in 1937 on a tour of the United States.

BELOW AND DETAILS RIGHT A labor of love: a hand-knitted cardigan with a satin-stitch embroidered yoke with patterning derived from western European folk motifs. The ground fabric has relief stripes of six stitch cables running vertically to match those on the sleeve.

British Knitwear Manufacturers

The day that war was declared, trade with continental Europe virtually ceased altogether and the home market in Britain collapsed – severe rationing was to be part of everyone's life for most of the following decade. Additional problems were caused by the majority of the knitting machinery and machine parts being imported from Germany, again improvisation and ingenuity were required for ad hoc repairs. In addition, the cashmere supply from China was negligible, as was the Australian wool that represented the bulk of production supplies.

As with most manufacturing industries, British label John Smedley had to comply with government regulations during the Second World War and turn over some of the manufacturing capability to produce uniforms, including the officers' Warnorm shirt in 1943 (see page 80). The Warnorm scheme was a program for limiting the felting shrinkage of knitwear garments supplied for the services. Leslie Banister was now the designer at the helm, and he deployed "cut and sew" techniques with double jersey to fashion tailored jackets with padded shoulders that displayed an obvious uniform influence (see also page 75). The company now started manufacturing "cut and sew" garments, which were not only cheaper and required less skill in manufacture, but also allowed for greater design ingenuity, with innovative seaming and darting. The color palette was appropriately somber: maroon, navy and gray.

Production slowed at Pringle of Scotland to the extent that the factory was closed for one week in four, yet surprisingly, after a few months of the "phoney war," the market in America picked up notably. The year 1939 proved most profitable with turnover exceeding expectations and the greatest number of exports going to Argentina and Uruguay. A certain amount of the production of these companies was still concerned with non-Utility knitwear, as government contracts sustained the skills of the workforce and made high-class knitwear newly affordable, resulting in increasing profits.

By the time supplies of wool had dried up completely, the end of the war was in sight and the Scottish knitwear manufacturers found that North America was desperate to import high-quality British goods. In 1947 head designer Otto Weisz declared that Pringle of Scotland was the bestselling brand of knitwear in the United States.

BELOW Staff at work in the export stock room at Robert Pringle & Son Ltd's factory in Hawick on the Scottish Borders, May 5, 1949. Here, orders for the finished garments were assembled, checked and made ready for dispatch to customers. By 1950 73 percent of Pringle's production was exported overseas, mostly to America.

ABOVE A plain, functional wool cardigan manufactured by John Smedley. The neckline buttoned high on the throat was a consistent feature of wartime knitwear, created in an effort to keep warm in the days of fuel rationing.

RIGHT Knitwear companies such as John Smedley found that the majority of their manufacturing output was taken up by government contracts to provide uniforms for the armed services. This Warnorm officer's vest in plated silk and merino wool dates from 1943. The method of production allowed minimal waste; the front and back consists of a single straight-knitted panel with ribs attached at each end. The neck opening is formed by cutting a semi-circle, the resulting flap then folded down and attached to the inside back neck.

LEFT A waist-length crewneck sweater with short sleeves in orange wool by John Smedley. The center of the front panel features pleats of gathered smocking stitch integrated into the fabric, using inlaid shirring elastic.

ABOVE This cardigan by John Smedley demonstrates detailed and complex pattern cutting in the topstitched shoulder detail, the gathers into the yoke and the puffed sleeves. A recurring detail in knitwear from the 1930s and 1940s is the center-front button band extending to the waist, which is then attached to a ribbed welt, resulting in a hybrid pullover/cardigan garment.

RIGHT British designer Mariah Luck-Szanto designed hand-knitted suits and dresses using stitches from Victorian patterns recommended for waistcoats as her inspiration. The knitted pieces were made up with conventional dressmaking techniques and proved popular until well into the 1950s. Here Szanto's Barbara dress in dark green hand-knitted Spintex dates from 1947.

The Hollywood Influence

Bob, why are men so crazy about sweater girls?
I don't know Judy, that's one mystery I'd like to unravel.

Judy Garland to Bob Hope,
U.S. Command Performance, 1942

Hollywood, as ever, provided light relief in troublesome times. During the 1940s the cinema produced two role models for women: stars such as Joan Crawford and Barbara Stanwyck represented the hardworking ambitious career woman struggling to make her way in a "man's world." In contrast was the voluptuous "Sweater Girl," the pin-up of the armed forces – actresses Jane Russell and later Marilyn Monroe were prime examples, exemplifying the look. Donald Spoto in his biography of Monroe describes a visit by her to Camp Pendleton to entertain the troops. Marilyn Monroe, wearing a figure-hugging cashmere sweater, was praised as "the most beautiful Sweater Girl" ever seen at the base: "She turned to the audience and said, 'You fellows down there are always whistling at Sweater Girls. I don't get all the fuss. Take away the sweaters and what have you got?'"

The answer was significant *embonpoint* harnessed in the pointed conical bras of the era. Brand names Maidenform, Berlei, Triumph and the British Marks & Spencer bras under the St. Michael label all constructed underwear that provided the desirable pneumatic silhouette.

The queen of the Sweater Girl look was Lana Turner, an American actress famously discovered at the age of 16 in the Top Hat Café on Sunset Boulevard. She first found fame in Mervyn LeRoy's *They Won't Forget*, a garish potboiler set in the Deep South. Although released in 1937, the film was immensely influential for women's fashion throughout America in the 1940s. The sweater in question was a scandalously figure-hugging one that delineated every curve and presented her breasts to the world. Lana Turner was at the height of her popularity during the Second World War – with women copying her style and fighting men adorning their planes and garrison walls with her image. She even had a plane named after her – the B-17 Tempest Turner.

American designers were quick to incorporate decorative elements in knitwear, even embellishing ready-made imported garments. Claire Potter's collection from 1940 included sweaters embroidered with beads and silk threads, and in 1941 Mainbocher jazzed up plain knits and made them into eveningwear to match his gowns by sewing on lace trim, beads, sequins and velvet appliqué. He also designed evening sweater dresses in shirred and draped synthetic jersey.

OPPOSITE Designing directly onto the figure by cutting and draping, pinning and basting was the preferred method of working by American designer Clare Potter, evidenced by this 1946 jersey dinner dress with fluted hemline.

BELOW When actress Lana Turner wore a tight-fitting sweater in the film *They Won't Forget,* she heralded the return of the hourglass figure and convinced a generation of women that knitwear could be sexy, particularly when worn over a "point and push-up" bra.

ABOVE Dolman sleeves, which increase in width from the wrist to the shoulder and form a single unit with the body, provided a perfect canvas for a decorated yoke. The body and yoke are cut to produce the star-shaped seam, emphasized by beadwork. Radial pintucks on the yoke match the star pattern.

THIS PAGE Photographed in 1949, this relaxed, yet elegant jersey shirt and longer-length plaid pleated skirt by Carolyn Schnurer shows fashion on the cusp of change. The military-inspired masculine silhouette is evolving into the feminine, yet unfussy look of 1950s American sportswear. The broad placket of the sweater, which has no buttons, leads to an exaggerated shirt collar, which together create a plunging V-neck. Accessorized with a knitted sailor cap and jewelry.

The American Knitwear Industry

In both America and Britain manufacturers increased their production capacity and manufacturing skills in response to the demand for the mass production of ready-to-wear fashion. With Europe at war, American manufacturers, specifically the International Ladies' Garment Workers' Union under the aegis of Julius Hochman, set out to make New York City the clothing capital of the world. It was estimated there were between 15 and 20 million customers available in Canada, and Central and South America. However, New York faced competition from several other regions in the United States. In 1941 California presented its own Fashion Futures, catwalk shows run by the Los Angeles and San Francisco regional Fashion Groups, which included the work of 75 designers, among them Irene Lentz and Gilbert Adrian.

For more than a century the Cleveland Garment District was one of the leading apparel manufacturing centers in the world. As well as being the location of the White Sewing Machine Company and the Standard Sewing Machine Company, later purchased by Singer, the district was home to many and various ready-to-wear manufacturers. These included several knitwear companies: the Dalton company, Majestic Knitwear, the Cleveland Worsted Mill Company, Federal Knitting and the Lion Knitting Mills, who became known for their Varsity or award-letter sweater. From the 1960s the company switched from wool to cotton manufacturing and began to produce sweaters for such retailers as Brooks Brothers, L. L. Bean and Saks Fifth Avenue.

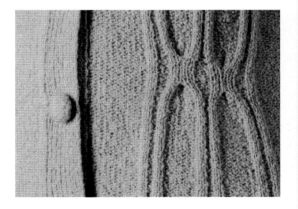

THIS PAGE A fully fashioned machine-knit suit in metallized thread from the U.S. The construction of the jacket deployed elaborate knitting methods, such as the shaped rib collar with reverse and convergent twin-spaced ribs to create an impression of soft tailoring. The raised rib motif continues on the knee-length skirt.

THIS PAGE The plain peplum and sleeves of this nipped-waist long cardigan are contrasted by the upper bodice and pockets at the hem. In these fancy purl panels, small diamond clusters of single stitches in pale blue add a delicate "powdered" pattern to the black ground.

OPPOSITE Refined post-war glamour in 1949 evoked by Elsa Schiaparelli's astrakhan jersey high-necked dress with raglan sleeves and draped front.

The Hadley Cashmere Company

One of the leading cashmere sweater manufacturers in the United States during the 1940s, the Hadley Cashmere Company produced cashmere and camelhair sweaters that were available in department stores across the country, either under the name of the company, identified by the label stitched into the side seam of the garment, or as knitwear commissioned by leading department stores. Hadley also sold knitted wool suits, which went on to achieve widespread commercial success with college girls in the 1950s. The Hadley cashmere sweaters were knitted in the solid colors seen on the Sweater Girls; they were also produced in complex intarsia designs – checks, animals, Argyles and other figurative or abstract patterns.

The Ohio Knitting Mills

Founded by Harry Stone in 1927, the Ohio Knitting Mills produced knitwear for 76 years with three generations of the Stone-Rand family running it. The knitwear they made was aimed at the same market as Hadley – to be sold in department stores throughout the U.S., including Saks Fifth Avenue. Commission knitting was undertaken for superior labels such as Pendleton, Van Heusen and Jack Winter.

The company was a massive institution in Cleveland, Ohio, taking up a whole city block and employing 1,000 workers at its peak. The diversity of their productions meant that demand was constant across the market – from high-end "designer" sweaters to mass-produced plain everyday tops. Aware of the need to keep their innovative designs for prosperity, from the late 1940s onwards the company began to archive key designs. This vast collection of remarkable design artifacts, representing mainstream fashion from the 1940s to the 1970s, is currently being revisited by the company and sold commercially.

RIGHT A selection of knitted menswear from the archives of the Ohio Knitting Mills. From top: Jacquard Grin-through wool knit, 1947; Raschel warp-knit wool pullover 1948; Raschel warp-knit cotton poorboy, 1944; Raschel warp-knit cotton polo shirt, 1950.

THIS PAGE Photographed in New York in 1949 by Genevieve Naylor, the dropped shoulderline of this three-quarter-length dolman-sleeved sweater designed by Majestic encapsulates the feminine, rounded silhouette of Christian Dior's New Look. The waist is emphasized by the belted skirt, designed by M. Sloat.

American Sportswear

During the war years America's fashion industry experienced the burgeoning of its home-grown talent, including Norman Norell and Claire McCardell, both of whom honed their skills under the aegis of Hattie Carnegie, the best-known ready-to-wear designer in the U.S. In 1941 McCardell produced a range of "playclothes" that in their simplicity and boldness presaged the Beat look a decade later. The range included a short dress of red striped wool jersey worn over skin-fitting red wool jersey underpants; fringed wool tartan shorts; a knitted wool pinafore teamed with a polka-dot shirt and shorts; and a wool wrap skirt worn with a turtleneck jersey top. Collars extended into cowls or hoods, often topstitched in contrasting colors.

Knitted jersey was also utilized by wholesale designer Joset Walker, who specialized in easy-wear, easy-launder drawstring-waisted dresses. French-born Walker, a classmate of Claire McCardell at Parson's School of Design, began her career in the "theatrical department" at Saks Fifth Avenue, then became a costume designer for R.K.O. Studios in the 1930s, before designing for dress manufacturer David Goodstein in 1940 and starting Joset Walker Designs.

Californian manufacturers such as Jantzen and Koret, founded in San Francisco in 1938 by Joseph and Stephanie Koret, were others who epitomized a relaxed West Coast aesthetic with ready-to-wear separates of mix-and-match pieces such as trousers, cardigan suits, wool ribbed turtle- and half-turtlenecked sweaters and sweater sets.

Clothes worn for sporting activities, as opposed to sportswear (known as leisurewear in the U.K.) were also in demand. Skiing was becoming an increasingly popular activity in the 1940s, with a dress code that was subject to fashionable trends. In 1941 *Vogue* invoked a "growing intolerance for anything but classic simplicity in ski clothes." Ever innovative, Elsa Schiaparelli designed a knitted ski top made backless for tanning purposes by a strip that rolled down into a military-style waist pack. The narrow silhouette included proofed gabardine ski trousers, which were slim-fitting and generally black, livened up by decorative Norwegian sweaters.

OPPOSITE American wholesale designer Joset Walker provided medium-priced fashion in the country's rapidly developing ready-to-wear market. Here her draped and pleated sweater in post-war pastels date from 1949.

RIGHT Model Janet Stevenson is ready for action in Quebec 1946. Her ski-wear ensemble of chunky woollen balaclava and two-by-two ribbed hand-knit sweater with an applied cable detail and matching balaclava is accessorized with aviator sun shades and leather gloves.

The Award-Letter Sweater

With the advent of organized sports in universities, the teams needed some sort of garment that identified them as a group and also signified athletic achievement. The concept of the unifying garment to be worn off the pitch or field originated at Harvard University in the late nineteenth century. "H" for "Harvard" was an embroidered design on a flannel shirt, rather than a knitted garment, and was given out only to those who played in the university sports teams, notably the 1891 "nine" baseball team. By the twentieth century the varsity sweater had replaced the shirt. As with most Ivy League trends, the practice was copied by other universities and colleges wishing to emulate the elite, and this in turn filtered down to the high-school level.

The award letter is usually made in the colors and initials representing the school attended and in the 1930s the sweater was partnered by leather-sleeved, wool-bodied jackets. In time the "letterman" sweater was also awarded to students in other fields of excellence – whether it be musical, performing arts or other academic achievements. An entire lexicon of symbols, colors and emblems appeared, all of which were either knitted into the sweater or embroidered once the student had achieved more awards. The student was only ever awarded the letter once, after which further significant achievements were signified by the addition of stripes on the arm or emblems around the original letter.

As a decorative clothing item, the varsity letter has a huge number of variations and no set standard is made to any school on how it should look, but vintage value depends on the age and rarity of the garment.

Norwegian Knitwear

Knitting has always been a vital skill in the countries of Northern Europe as the harsh climate and the rugged terrain, only suitable for raising sheep, rendered knitted garments necessary for survival. In Norway, the earliest sweaters were initially items of underwear for men which were worn over a shirt and tucked into trousers, with a waistcoat (vest) and coat over the top. Many of the sweaters featured the country's typical two-color design with the lower part of the sweater left unpatterned as it was unseen. What is thought of as the archetypal ski sweater is a two-stranded pattern which came into fashion around 1830, depending on the region.

Patterning of clothing, whether woven or knitted, is a significant way for a culture to express its identity and carry its history forward into the future. The double-strand knitting also had a practical purpose: it provided warmth and durability, as well as being decorative. The Selbu star, sometimes called the Norwegian star or snowflake (though a snowflake has six points), was the first two-color work to appear in Norway. Other motifs included the eight-petal flowers, called *attebladroser*, various floral motifs and initials. Animal imagery included reindeer, making the Norwegian knitted sweater particularly appropriate wear for the American tradition of the Christmas sweater.

Mittens have a great cultural significance in Norway. The tradition of "unpacking the mittens" at the onset of winter is a ritual that dates back to the Middle Ages, when time was tracked using a calendar stick or *primstav*. The Nordic people used a lunar calendar to divide the year into two portions: summer began on April 14 and winter on October 14. In the two-sided calendar, the summer side had the image of a tree, the winter side a picture of mittens. Mittens would have smaller patterns on the palm for durability and larger patterns on the backs of the hands. The cuffs would be ribbed for boys and lace for girls.

The circular knitting needle was probably developed in Norway. It was advertised as Flexiknit, patent applied for, in *"Ladies' field" Jumpers* (Book 1) in 1924. The flexible part was made of steel-wire cable and the rigid ends were crimped on. The joins tended to snag the knitted yarn; later developments used plastic or aluminum. Carrying the yarn over the right hand seems to be the oldest method of working in Western Europe; carrying the yarn over the left hand originated in Germany. An article in *Vestlandske Kunstindustrimuseum Arbok* 1954–57 states this practice was introduced to Norway by upper-class knitters during the nineteenth century and passed on to the artisan class. At the same time, the Norwegian word *binde* gave way to the German *strikke* as the customary term for knitting.

There are common elements between the knitting patterns and techniques of Shetland and Norway; ever since the Viking occupations there was close contact between the two countries and they spoke mutually understandable languages. Although both knitwear traditions utilize the eight-pointed Norwegian star, it did not become dominant in Shetland until the 1940s. In America, the distinctive patterns and techniques of Norwegian knitting became familiar as immigrants took their skills with them to the Midwest – it was particularly important as a member of an immigrant community to retain the patterns and culture of their homeland. In the Midwest Norwegian immigrants raised sheep, sheared them, carded the wool and spun it into yarn. Spinning wheels could be purchased from mail-order companies such as Alfred Andresen & Company of Minneapolis, Minnesota, who imported wheels from Norway.

BELOW Photographed in New Hampshire in 1946 aboard the first peacetime ski train of the Boston & Maine Railroad, these skiing enthusiasts learn the art of waxing skis from instructor Erick Ekberg. All their sweaters feature variations of the Selbu star motif, sometimes referred to as the "snowflake pattern."

▶ Knitted jackets

Intimations of Carmen Miranda, America's highest-paid entertainer of the era, appear in this exotic flower-bedecked turban and maquillage. Dating from 1941, the hand-crocheted short jacket is elevated out of the realms of the ordinary by the use of gold yarn and elbow-length gloves.

▲ Hand-knits and homemade

Hand-knitting flourished during clothes rationing in the wartime period of "make do and mend." This twinset dating from 1949 has all the features common to the time, including the short waist, high neckline and numerous buttons.

◀ The Sweater Girl look

Form-fitting pastel-colored sweaters in fluffy fibers such as mohair and angora had popular appeal to the newly emerging teenager, as in this hand-knitted ribbed sweater with set-in sleeves dating from 1949.

Key looks of the decade

1940s

Military styling

"Uniform" colors of gray, navy and maroon were popular, as were patriotic motifs. Short-waisted cardigans to wear under uniforms and V-neck sleeveless waistcoats became appropriate for both sexes and added much-needed warmth.

Shoulder pads

Women's fashions became more masculine and structured, particularly in jackets and coats, which were enhanced by a padded shoulder. The strong shoulderline appeared in sweaters, dresses and even lingerie.

American leisurewear

During the interwar years the American fashion industry achieved a recognizable identity of its own, of which knitted separates were an essential component. The exponents of these informal and practical ready-to-wear fashions included Clare Potter and Claire McCardell.

▲ Tailored and fitted

The tailored sophistication of this chrome-gray fitted wool jersey cardigan with softly gathered gray flannel skirt and snood by B. H. Wragge epitomizes the postwar importance placed on meticulous grooming and matching accessories that began with Dior's New Look in 1947.

▶ Draped jersey

Eveningwear provided an elegant counterpoint to the Utility fashions. A recurring theme was full-length dresses in fluid draped jersey inspired by classical Greek statuary. This column of draped and knotted silk jersey is in the style of Madam Grès and enlivened by costume jewelry.

1950s:
Fully Fashioned

During the 1950s knitwear became a valuable asset to every woman's wardrobe. Although still inherently practical, it resolutely held its own in the new era of luxuriousness heralded by Parisian couturier Christian Dior's radical Corolle line of 1947. This was instantly dubbed the "New Look" by fashion journalists and celebrated the return of the hourglass figure, in contrast to the masculine silhouette of wartime clothes. From the short, skimpy skirts of Utility wear, a government-prescribed uniform for civilians, hemlines were lowered to within 12 in (30 cm) of the floor as Dior's models swept along the catwalk of his salon on Avenue Montaigne. The broad-shouldered jacket was replaced by a sloping shoulderline and tiny waists encased in the internal corsets of the garments were emphasized by skirts consisting of yards of stiffened fabric. This revolutionary look was a backlash against the years of restraint and clothes worn for function, not fun. A fashion press more used to recommending unraveling old cardigans in order to reknit new sweaters (as *Vogue* had done during the war) seized on the New Look with unparalleled excitement.

The New Look was commercially successful and spearheaded the revival of Paris as the center of fashion once more. As the decade progressed the silhouette became less extreme and clothing less contoured to the body. Chanel reopened her house in 1954; she viewed Dior's "crinolinization" of women with anathema, and persisted with her relaxed pared-down aesthetic of wearable suits with hemlines falling to just below the knee. The simple construction and shape of these suits made them easy to copy by manufacturers, and although the fabrics and detailing were inferior to the bespoke garments, they provided an affordable elegance for the consumer. In 1957 Parisian couturier Balenciaga produced the chemise dress, which redefined the silhouette once again. Hubert de Givenchy opened his couture house in 1952, and in 1957 he further freed women from the tyrannical waspie and corset with the introduction of his Sack dress, a forerunner of the simple shifts of the following decade.

Daytime Decorum

Christian Dior's designs had an immediate impact on knitwear designers, who responded to the desire for feminine, figure-enhancing clothes. The high-necked, high-waisted cardigans and pullover sweaters of the wartime years gave way to low-buttoning cardigans with the softly rounded raglan or more extreme batwing or dolman sleeves replacing the padded set-in sleeves. Cardigans and pullovers now fell to the hip, in keeping with the longer skirt length. Dyes were once again available, and pastel colors were popular after the somber tones of the previous decade. There were now more yarn qualities from which to choose, including double knit and four-ply, which gave a sturdier fabric suitable for the burgeoning leisurewear market.

High fashion celebrated the elegant grown-up woman, with the emphasis on grooming and a ladylike demeanor. Good taste triumphed, and accessories had to be appropriate for the occasion unless the woman wanted to suffer social disapprobation. The twinset exemplified faultless female decorum. Feminine, but not sexy: that was the remit of the Hollywood Sweater Girls. Easy to clean and versatile, the Scottish twinset was a vital item in every woman's wardrobe. Worn with a tailored suit, or a skirt woven from matching yarn, the twinset could be dressed up with pearls and the new pointed stiletto heels, or dressed down with capri pants and ballet flats, a look popularized by the gamine film star and fashion icon Audrey Hepburn.

British women, however, were denied their twinsets in cashmere and had to make do with lambswool or merino wool. In 1950, the sale of cashmere goods to the British market was prohibited, and all cashmere products from the Scottish manufacturers had to be exported to America. Strained relations between America and China meant that cashmere had to be sourced from Russia, as Chinese cashmere was embargoed by the American government.

PAGE 96 Photographed in 1956 by Richard Rutledge, the full skirt, white blouse and formal red cardigan with gold buttons are designed by Greta Plattry. The cardigan is hand-knitted in fancy rib wool, running from cuff to cuff, as the dolman sleeve seamlessly grows into the body and then tapers back again to finish at the opposite wrist.

RIGHT Founded by Robert Pringle in 1815, Pringle of Scotland is one of the oldest global luxury goods brands. During the 1950s the order books of the label were overflowing and demand exceeded supply for their cashmere sweaters. This pale pink short-sleeved sweater, styled along the lines of Christian Dior's New Look, is partnered with a voluminous gathered skirt.

Pringle make sweaters lovelier

It's not only the *name* that tells you

it's a Pr

PRINGLE OF SCOTLAND

American college girls took pride in their "cashmere collection," and couldn't get enough of these luxurious garments. Demand soon exceeded supply, a growing problem for the Hawick knitwear manufacturers owing to their position in the rural Scottish borders where the work force was limited. A technical breakthrough by Bentley Cotton in 1955 increased production dramatically: the Automatic Rib Transfer Attachment was a machine that attached the rib automatically to the garment, a process previously undertaken by hand. A single machine could now produce 650 garments a week.

Products from companies sited in the Scottish borders, such as Ballantyne, Pringle, Hogg of Hawick, Dalkeith and Lyle & Scott, had a reputation for quality unmatched by competitors in America or England. The latter preferred the more economical option of manufacturing long runs of the same garment and were less prepared to do shorter runs in diverse styles, which required time-consuming and therefore expensive continual adjustments to the machine run. Scottish knitwear was "dyed in the wool" rather than after the yarn was spun, providing a greater saturated and even color tone, a more expensive process than the American system of knitting with undyed "white wool."

America's largest and most successful cashmere manufacturer was the Dalton and Hadley Knitwear Company of Cleveland (see also page 88), who manufactured 1,000,000 sweaters a year for the college girl. These were cheaper garments than the Scottish brands, but of a lesser quality. So high was the reputation of Scottish products that when Berhard Altmann of Vienna started manufacturing in the U.S., producing "American" cashmere, it was made in "Scots" styles, and even marketed under Scottish-sounding names such as Bonnie Briar. Scottish manufacturers were quick to capitalize and consolidate their popularity in America. Pringle's designer of the time, Otto Weisz, reported back from a fact-finding mission from the continent that the U.S. consumer required "tighter ribbed waists, better packaging envelopes, mothproofing, a wide choice of color and a spare button on each cardigan."

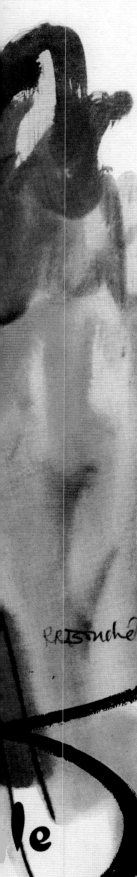

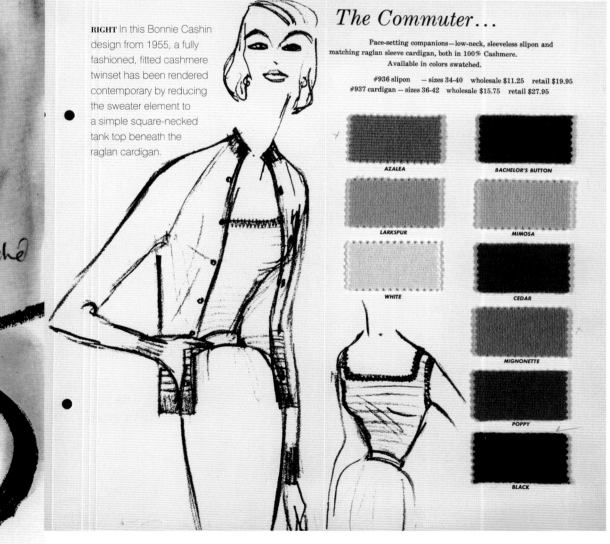

RIGHT In this Bonnie Cashin design from 1955, a fully fashioned, fitted cashmere twinset has been rendered contemporary by reducing the sweater element to a simple square-necked tank top beneath the raglan cardigan.

The Commuter...

Pace-setting companions—low-neck, sleeveless slipon and matching raglan sleeve cardigan, both in 100% Cashmere.
Available in colors swatched.

#936 slipon – sizes 34-40 wholesale $11.25 retail $19.95
#937 cardigan – sizes 36-42 wholesale $15.75 retail $27.95

AZALEA

BACHELOR'S BUTTON

LARKSPUR

MIMOSA

WHITE

CEDAR

MIGNONETTE

POPPY

BLACK

LEFT The pure Botany wool Hucklow sweater by John Smedley was manufactured in a range of colors, including japonica, beau blue, alpine pink, bracken and wisteria, as well as the red shown here. The fully-fashioned top has set-in short sleeves and an open V–neck with plackets, leading to a shaped shirt collar in 1x1 rib with raised ridges. These sporty ridges (ripple stitch, or *altzettina*) are achieved by retarding fabric production on one face of the fabric while continuing to add extra "single-bed" rows on the other face, before returning to normal 1x1 rib.

BELOW LEFT This short-sleeved, striped, fine-gauge top by John Smedley features the patented and unique three-button Isis poloneck, with the collar in a solid shade. The Bentley Cotton fully-fashioned frames that were used for body panel production at this time were limited to only three separate striping carriers, which created an interesting discipline for designers.

OPPOSITE Photographed in 1952, this coarse-gauge fitted sweater in moss stitch has a neat Peter Pan collar, trimmed with a band of 1x1 rib. This is contrasted by deep cuffs and hem in 2x2 rib, which is a more elastic structure. The sharp knitted top and upswept coiffure is teamed with a tonally striped pleat skirt, the whole completed by the distinctive accessories of the era: the oversized charm bracelet and the under-sized dog.

Embellished and Elegant

Twinsets and cardigans scaled heights of variety in color, texture and, above all, embellishment in the 1950s. The cardigan became not only a daytime staple, but also acceptable eveningwear. Validated by American couturier and designer Mainbocher as socially appropriate, cashmere silk-lined cardigans embellished with appliqué, beadwork or fur collars accessorized his elegant evening sheath dresses. Worn with a long silk or velvet skirt or slung around the shoulders of a cocktail dress, knitwear crossed the boundaries from sport to sparkle. At the lower end of the market, plain sweaters were bought in by manufacturers and then jazzed up with beading. American designers Pat Baldwin and Edith Salzman both designed covetable beaded cardigans, but Helen Bond Carruthers from Versailles, Kentucky, produced the most collectable cardigans of the 1950s. Recognizable by the label in the waistband and the cropped bolero style, these are rare and expensive.

Many sweaters, especially the highly decorated ones, were made in Hong Kong, which had a considerable knitwear manufacturing base during this period, producing not only cashmere but also lambswool and angora blends in fashionable styles. All of these garments were "fully fashioned," that is, knitted to shape, not cut and sewn. The majority of the embellished cardigans were made from noble fibers

such as cashmere or angora (see also pages 68–69). The fragility of these luxury yarns was occasionally strengthened with the addition of a small percentage of nylon by American companies, although this was a practice much frowned on by the traditional Scottish manufacturers as it was seen to diminish the quality of the product. Nylon was usually added as a fine polymer coating to the cashmere fibers, filling the spaces between the wool hair scales. Shrinkage is caused by these scales becoming tangled with wear and careless washing, so the addition of nylon helped to prevent matting and felting, but also made a significant difference to the luxurious handle of the garment.

LEFT AND BELOW Knitwear goes glamorous with this dolman-sleeved sweater, encrusted with pearlized beads and iridescent leaves. The deep U-shaped neckline has the potential to slip off the shoulder for extra impact. The central cascade of decoration also reinforces the emphasis on the décolleté.

OPPOSITE Attention to detail was a prerequisite of the grown-up glamour of the 1950s era, from the luxurious beaded cashmere sweater by Regina to the matching jewelry and perfect maquillage; in this case, Revlon's lipstick and nail polish branded Where's The Fire? Photographed in 1950 in New York by Frances McLaughlin-Gill.

ABOVE AND RIGHT
The sophistication and urbanity of Italian style was universally recognized in the 1950s. This sleeveless short-waisted top in angora was produced by the Luisa Spagnoli company in Perugia, Italy. The handworked nature of the crochet lace trimming around the boatneck recalls the early craft-oriented profile of the company as originally established by Luisa Spagnoli before her death in 1935. As well as being the first person and company to breed angora rabbits to produce yarns and knitted garments, Luisa Spagnoli is credited with the invention of a global confectionery product: "Baci Perugina." The fashion and knitwear brand continues to thrive today.

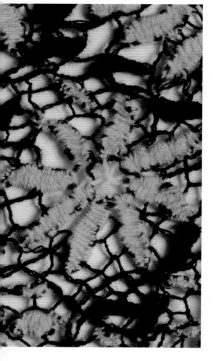

LEFT AND RIGHT Extravagant pastel decoration, hand-embroidered in wool satin stitch onto an openwork top, belies the simplicity of the underlying fabric and garment structure. The "scaffolding" of the garment is a basic crochet mesh in black wool, a structure akin to that used in some nets and string bags.

THIS PAGE A floral appliqué cashmere cardigan by Helen Bond Carruthers, the designer of the most collectable of the embroidered cashmere cardigans from this era. Her methods included recycling exquisite satin-stitch embroidery motifs from secondhand and vintage articles such as chinoiserie-inspired silk shawls and old Belgian bed linens. The cut-out fragments of pre-stitched cloth were then assembled onto plain cashmere cardigans and re-attached using appliqué embroidery. The finished garments were lined with silk chiffon to obscure the simplicity of the hybrid confection and to stabilize the behavior of the knitted article against distortion by the weight of the appliqué.

Ready-to-Wear

During the post-war period, factories both in America and Europe utilized the latest technology to supply a burgeoning mass-market. Ready-to-wear (*prêt-a-porter*) lines were initially developed by the couture houses who wished to offer a more expensive version of mass-produced garments. Knitwear was never subject to the same bespoke practices as couture, fittings were not necessary, and no machine could be set to produce a single bespoke garment. Once the couture houses realized the commercial possibilities of ready-to-wear, knitted garments came into their own and were increasingly subject to the design process, with all the hallmarks of the signature detailing of the couturier.

American ready-to-wear fashion became increasingly divorced from the European aesthetic, with an emphasis on sportswear. A very definable American style that had begun with the pioneering work of designers such as Claire McCardell now gained momentum, consolidated by Bonnie Cashin, who provided a modern sensibility with designs of loosely cut clothes with minimum seaming in natural fibers such as wool and cotton. Tourism was a popular activity now that the war was over, and Cashin responded to the need for easy-care fabrics that traveled well by utilizing knitted fabrics for her innovative concept of "layered dressing." The designer produced knitted dress and jacket ensembles that espoused a modern approach to the capsule wardrobe.

Sportswear also continued to include the knitted swimsuit. In spite of the obvious drawbacks, designers such as Tina Leser utilized knitting for maillots and two-piece bathing suits, the latter worn with a white calico bra under the knitted bolero. "Playsuits" entered the fashion lexicon: all-in-one shorts suits, midriff-baring sweaters and brassière tops were produced, often in a combination of knitted jersey and other "humble" fabrics such as denim or chambray.

ABOVE RIGHT Layered dressing by Bonnie Cashin from Joseph Guttman, featuring a combined hood and gilet in "full-cardigan stitch" worn over a narrow knitted dress with simple stripe detailing at the upper arm – denoting the architectural relationship with the sleeveless top. The slipover, which has a four-button opening and a change of rib at the midriff, is styled with a contrasting leather cinch belt.

RIGHT "The Resorter" by Bonnie Cashin, a two-ply sweater in rack stitch with a ribbed, grown-on hood. The needle set-out of the knitting machine has been adjusted at the midriff to produce a wider rib that has greater elasticity and will generate the nipped-in look the designer intends.

ABOVE This Bonnie Cashin sketch indicates a plain knit top that is soft and slim with trimmed cap sleeves, tucked into the girdled waist of a full skirt. The contrast trim at the plunge neck with its stand-up collar adds the subtle formality of a bound revere, chiming with the business-like bucket bag.

No. 819

The Resorter...

Two-ply rack stitch pullover with ribbed hood. Long sleeves. Fleur-de-lis brass-buttoned neck opening. Waistline shaping achieved by means of wide ribbing. Available in colors swatched.
#819 slipon – sizes 36-40   wholesale $11.25   retail $19.95

CRIMSON

WHITE

SAPPHIRE

BLACK

LIGHT BLUE

THIS PAGE The long, lean silhouette of this 1951 double-jersey wool dress was an alternative to the hourglass full-skirted figure of Dior's New Look. Couture cutting is evident in the manipulation of the grown-on collar emerging from a small U-shaped yoke, its curves replicated in the inset pockets at the hip. A single button fastens the invisible fly-fronted jacket.

The Sweater Dress and the Hand Knit

An elongated version of the figure-hugging sweaters worn by Hollywood stars, the "sweater dress" delineated every curve from neck to mid calf. However, the potential for loucheness was nullified by the armory of foundation garments worn beneath, customary no matter how slender the body. Boat-shaped necklines, or even an off-the-shoulder, wide, rolled collar, together with a short raglan sleeve, comprised the most seductive of these garments. The sweater dress provided uncomplicated one-stop dressing, and was beaded and embroidered around the neckline for evening, or dressed down with a patterned silk scarf tied around the neck and accessorized by walking shoes for daytime. With the increasing introduction of synthetic fibers such as Orlon and Acrilan into their manufacture, the dresses became lighter and easier to care for, though static would always remain a problem.

As the decade progressed, the chemise, or "sheath" dress, inspired by couturiers Dior and Balenciaga, translated into a more relaxed version of the sweater dress. Textured yarns – particularly bouclé – were favored for their dense texture and ability to hold their shape. American designers such as Joseph Guttman mass-produced sweater dresses, but hand-knit yarn manufacturers, eager to seize on every trend, provided patterns for the ambitious home-knitter, sometimes with unfortunate results. As hand-knitting is less densely textured than machine knitting, fashionable soon became frumpy as the knitted fabric bagged around the hips after wear.

Patons & Baldwins

Supplying wool for domestic use was big business and a thriving industry. One of the major suppliers was Patons & Baldwins, now part of Coates Crafts, which also includes Rowan yarns and Jaeger hand-knits.

The company's origin lay in the mid-eighteenth century, when James Baldwin of Halifax, England, and John Paton of Alloa, Scotland, independently developed businesses working in the yarn-spinning industry. Several generations later the two companies amalgamated to form Patons & Baldwins Ltd. in 1920. The trademarks "Baldwins Beehive" and "Patons Rose" became synonymous with fashion quality. By 1955 the company claimed to have the "World's Biggest Knitting Wool Factory," based at Darlington, England, which included 40 acres of buildings and 2½ miles of private railway. A complete list of P&B Wools for the home-knitter included: classic Botany wools; "Patonized," in two-, three- and four-ply; vest wool; and baby wool. Fancy wools included crepe and bouclet. Patons' Nylox knitting wool was a combination of Botany wool and nylon. One of the new synthetics, rayon, also

BELOW LEFT Bonnie Cashin was a pioneer of American sportswear and proponent of "layered" dressing that exploited the properties of knitted fabrics to accommodate the lifestyle of the modern, working woman. She used the sensitivities and resonances of the Modern movement in architecture as a lexicon for her approach to the composition and proportioning of relationships between layers, forms, materials and colors. Her layered outfits have the rigor of soft architecture brought close to the functioning modern body. The seamless opulent ribbed shrug here is a counterpoint to the delicate kid mohair jersey dress, which has a subtle band of contrast color, announcing the location of the pockets in the seam.

LEFT Simplicity in the relationship of volumes and materials is a signature of the Bonnie Cashin philosophy, however the designer had the ability to bring a lightness of touch to her collections too. This elegant travel suit in jersey, framed geometrically by dark bindings, is accessorized by a banded straw hat and wicker luggage. It is all cylinders, rectangles and lines, mixed with materials.

appeared in the list and Patons also offered Fuzzy-Wuzzy angora and beryl angora.

P&B, recognizable by their logo of initials inside the outline of a beehive, produced an annual digest. Each issue contained various tips by James Norbury, "television's knitting man and chief designer to Patons and Baldwins Ltd." These exhortations included the following tips:

◆ BUY WOOL WISELY: You must have the right material to work with. Where soft texture and the subtlest colours are called for – as with baby clothes and fashion designs – choose Botany wool. Make sure your garment will be the same shade throughout by buying all the wool you need at one go.

◆ NEEDLES: Long needles are best for really even knitting. The correct gauge of needle is linked up with the very important subject of TENSION.

◆ When you put your knitting away for some hours, stop at the end of a row, and always join in a new ball of wool at the end of a row.

◆ More garments are spoiled by bad MAKING UP, than by any other fault.

As machine-knitting technology became increasingly complex, the gap between the hand-knitted and the manufactured garment grew ever wider. Hand-knitted garments were not perceived as sophisticated, and there was no pride in the craft of knitting. The process still suffered from the utilitarian attitude towards knitting left over from the 1940s "make do and mend" mentality, which made a virtue of necessity. No matter how advanced the pattern, or expert the making up, fashion knitwear belonged to the realms of the machine-made. It was not until the following decade that the craft of hand-knitting was valued for its own sake and the virtues of the idiosyncratic handcrafted garment appreciated.

BBC TELEVISION'S "MR KNITTING" TIPS FOR WASHING HAND-KNITS

The tips below from James Norbury, which appeared in one of the P&B publications, are still relevant today.

Washing hand-knits needs care if a garment is to keep its shape. There are three stages.

1 **Washing:** Dissolve completely a little soap in hot water and add cold until the suds are only warm. Detergents (not bleaches) can be used, especially in a hard-water area. Before their first wash, steep all-white garments for 30 minutes in cold water containing 3 to 4 tablespoons of household ammonia. White sweaters with other colours must not be treated in this way. Put the woolly in and work the suds through it gently and quickly with the hands – two minutes will usually be ample depending on the size and condition of the garment. Use only warm water. If it is too hot for your elbow, it is much too hot for woollies. Don't rub the garment. Don't lift it above the surface of the water. Don't leave it to soak.

2 **Rinsing:** After washing and during rinsing, support your woolly with both hands whenever you lift it from the water. Rinse in two changes of warm water, or until the water runs clear and there are no more soap bubbles. Remove every trace of soap. A few drops of white vinegar in the final water are good for coloured garments.

3 **Drying:** Squeeze the garment between towels, or fold in a towel and pass through a light rubber wringer, removing any buttons that may cut the fabric. Don't pull or twist the garment – don't leave it laying in a heap. Ease the garment back to its original size and shape, and dry flat away from excessive heat. Don't hang it up – don't try to dry it too quickly in front of the fire or in the sun.

The Beat Goes On

Daytime decorum and grown-up glamour began to be eroded towards the end of the decade, when, for the first time in fashion history, young people rebelled against wearing the same clothes as their parents. A separate market began catering specifically for the burgeoning numbers of teenagers who were beginning to define a style unique to them. For the American bobbysoxer this included tight-fitting short-sleeved pullover sweaters or cardigans in baby blue and pink. These were worn over pointed bras and with bouffant skirts supported by layers of stiffened petticoats. As an early act of teenage sartorial rebellion, knitted cardigans were worn back to front.

Rebellious teenagers discarded the form-fitting twinset or sweetheart-line sweater altogether because of its associations with the older generation. They wore instead the "sloppy joe," an oversized sweater with a rolled collar, hem and cuffs, occasionally appropriated from a father's or boyfriend's wardrobe, along with his shirt. Falling loosely around the body, almost to the knees, it was worn with rolled-up denim jeans and saddle shoes.

A more subversive look was inspired by the Beat movement, the avant-garde poets and novelists led by Jack Kerouac, who favored the black polo-neck knitted sweater, worn with denim jeans as popularized by Marlon Brando in *The Wild One* (1953). This aesthetic crossed the Atlantic from New York's Greenwich Village to emerge in the jazz clubs and cafes of the bohemian Left Bank in Paris and was the initial inspiration for Mary Quant's "Chelsea Look" in London.

In 1955 the trail-blazing boutique Bazaar opened on the King's Road in Chelsea. Mary Quant played with the proportions and gender of fashion garments as she scaled up cardigans into dresses, dropped the V-neck of a sweater to the waist and redefined a man's classic three-button football sweater into a dress to be worn with colored tights. Most striking was her use of color. She juxtaposed plum with ginger, pale blue and maroon, tobacco brown with purple and mustard with navy.

This was essentially a London look, expensive and difficult to access for the average teenager until the following decade when an expansion of the boutique movement resulted in the regional specialist shops selling their version of what was deemed "cool." Meanwhile the Teds roamed the streets of British cities – flashy, predatory and every mother's nightmare. A pastiche of the New Edwardians – an upper-class version of the Edwardian dandy – the Teds had a uniform of crepe-soled "brothel creepers" and knee-length jackets with velvet collars worn with a shoestring tie. Their girlfriends wore neon oversized mohair sweaters with the V of the neckline slipping from one shoulder, with shrunk-fit jeans, ballet flats and a cigarette smoldering in the corner of an unmade-up mouth. Although the original mohair sweaters were expensive imports from Italy, teenage girls often grappled with outsize needles and double-knit yarn in a first attempt at knitting to replicate the look.

The growing numbers of college students in Britain had none of the preppy smartness of their American counterpart. Baggy corduroy trousers were topped by thick cable-knit sweaters worn under duffle coats and a long multi-striped scarf. These chunky sweaters, often hand-knitted, were occasionally patterned in versions of Aran knit or Tyrolean style.

LEFT Photographed by Frank Pocklington for the *Picture Post* in September 1955, tapered dark "slacks" are teamed with a long and loose rib jacquard sweater. The sculptured high collar, long cuffs and hem trim, in solid shade 2x1 rib, add definition within the silhouette. Two-color patterning is reminiscent of the Indonesian decorative dyeing technique of batik.

Folk Fashions

American and European society became more mobile after the Second World War. Tourist destinations such as Paris, Rome and London and the ephemera of travel all provided inspiration for the vogue for novelty sweaters. The French poodle had a particular place in the iconography of youthful aspirations; it represented a European sophistication and adorned a plethora of items, from printed fabrics and handbags to jewelry, knitwear and the "poodle" skirt. The silhouette of the dog would be applied to the garment, including very often an actual miniature collar and lead.

The exotic also had an appeal, and there was a trend for peasant-inspired clothing such as dirndl skirts and off-the-shoulder blouses featuring ornate prints inspired by ethnic patterning. Matching sweaters in bright primary colors incorporated embroidery, appliqué and rickrack braiding or even found objects such as small shells. Textured surfaces were popular, particularly the bobble stitch; matching bobbles would be attached to the drawstring threaded through the neck of the garment. These were worn with homemade circular skirts in felt, decorated with appliquéd motifs, often representing images from contemporary music such as the double clef, musical notes or guitars. Other circular skirts were manufactured with printed scenes of exotic places.

Tyrolean knitting

The fad for textured decorative knitwear included the techniques of Scandinavian countries as well as other European traditions. In 1956, in his *Encyclopaedia of Knitting,* James Norbury invented the name "Tyrolean" knitting to describe cable and bobble patterns that were ornamented with embroidery. These were constructed in heavy wool, generally in white or cream. The Tyrol is a region of southern Austria with a tradition of knitting stockings with intricate ribbing, cabling and interlacing of ribs, and although no body garments were constructed in this style before the twentieth century, the technique became popular with hand-knitters in the 1950s. Often featuring an overall design of a small motif, such as the four-stitch cross worked in two colors to form a small fleur-de-lis, other designs featured popular imagery such as the reindeer and snowflake. Tyrolean knitting is close in style to that of other northern European countries.

BELOW AND OPPOSITE This voluminous Nordic-style cardigan in navy and ecru wool is decorated in slipstitch with elements from the geometric repeat patterns used to signify Scandinavian origin. The eight-point star recalls the snowflake, while the powdered grid of single white stitches suggests a flurry of snow falling. The garment panels are fully fashioned, but deviate only slightly from the rectangular. Collar and button bands are rendered durable and festive by the attachment, with gold thread, of a concentric band of reversed slipstitch patterning, where the floating yarns in red and green give the appearance of a woven wool ribbon.

The Argyle Check

The 1950s heralded the heyday of the Argyle check, particularly in America, where it became a wardrobe staple of men's leisurewear. The provenance of the Argyle lies in the tartan hose worn by men with the Scottish kilt. Originally cut and sewn from woven cloth, the tartan was cut on the bias, so that the diagonal pattern ran around the leg. By the nineteenth century woven versions had been replaced by hose, hand-knitted by the intarsia technique – a method of patternmaking deploying the use of two or more colors within the same course on weft-knitted plain, rib or purl fabrics. (The word "intarsia" originates from the creation of patterns by wood inlay called *intersio,* a technique brought to Italy in the fifteenth century from the Middle East by the Certosini monks.)

The Argyle check proved popular with the golfing set of the 1920s, led by the influential fashionista, the Duke of Windsor. When knitting machine manufacturers Dubied released the 00 intarsia knitting machines in the 1950s to the market, traditional knitwear manufacturers such as Pringle revived the pattern to great commercial success. The design of elongated diamonds in two or more colors overlaid by a linear check, called "rakers" in Scotland, was largely exploited as signifying a "classic" or "preppy" reference until appropriated by avant-garde designer Vivienne Westwood, who deconstructed the design in the 1980s.

ARTIFICIAL FIBERS

From the 1950s onwards knitwear increasingly included manufactured fibers. There are two varieties of artificial fibers, manmade and synthetic.

Acrylic (Orlon): A synthetic based on coal, water, petroleum and limestone, acrylic yarn attempts to replicate the feel and properties of wool. Relatively inexpensive to manufacture, acrylic yarn is now used for cheaper knitwear only. However, in the 1960s it was seen as a modern, easy-care fiber that was eagerly appropriated by contemporary designers. Like most knitted synthetic yarns, it pills on use and easily loses its shape.

Nylon: A member of the synthetic polyamide family, nylon is the strongest of all the fibers while still being light in weight. Useful for sportswear because of its strength, it is often mixed with more delicate fibers such as cashmere to add durability. Nylon stockings were introduced in America in 1939 as a substitute for silk, though their use was restricted with nylon being used in the production of parachutes. In the 1950s nylon was a new enough fiber to be heralded with excitement for its easy-to-care properties. As *Butterick Fashion News* of April 1950 claimed: "Although a great deal has been written and spoken about nylon, it still remains for many, a magic name. It is almost magical, of course, for it is very strong, quick to dry, light and beautiful. As a supporting fiber, nylon combines with other fibers such as cotton, silk, wool and rayon to make beautiful long-wearing fabrics in a variety of weights and textures."

Polyester: A polyner fiber composed of synthetic materials, polyester was introduced by DuPont in 1953. Widely used for budget garments, and often mixed with other fibers to make it more absorbent, it is wrinkle-free and doesn't lose its shape.

Rayon: Also known as artificial silk, Viscose, Acetate and Cupro, rayon was selected as the generic term for artificial silk in 1924, and had been in development since the 1880s. It was the first manmade fiber and is composed of regenerated cellulose or wood pulp. A popular substitute for silk in the 1930s, it was also used widely in the 1940s in synthetic seaters for its draping qualities. Early garments in rayon are not washable.

Spandex: During the Second World War scientists developed Spandex, a manmade substitute for rubber, since the raw material originated in enemy territory held by the Japanese. Also appearing under the names Elastane and Lycra, spandex is an elastic fiber and can be drawn out to 500 percent of its original length and still spring back into shape repeatedly, improving the fit of sportswear. A small percentage of Spandex is often incorporated into outerwear; 1 or 2 percent is enough for the garment to retain its shape.

▶ Dolman sleeve

The dolman sleeve was a recurring fashion detail during the 1950s, emphasizing the softly rounded feminine shoulder of Christian Dior's New Look. Here a boatneck, hand-knitted wool sweater with inset dolman sleeves is produced in "knickerbocker" yarn in a fancy rib, from 1958.

▶ Twinsets

Unrivaled for quality, and a paradigm of timeless good taste, the Scottish fully-fashioned cashmere twinset has proved a wardrobe staple since its inception in the 1930s. Those in pastel cashmere were most coveted: this one is from a 1950s Braemar catalog.

incomparably y[...]
fully fashion[...]
knitw[...]

Key looks of the decade
1950s

◀ Summer knits

The necessity for soignée sophistication even applied to summer clothes and resortwear as in this halter-necked, knitted cotton top designed by New York label Nelly de Grab in 1953.

Beaded cardigans

The popularity of the embellished cardigan represented the transition of knitwear from a daytime staple to evening elegance. Promoted by American label Bender & Hamburger as "Costume Intime," this line included a full circular velvet skirt teamed with a low-cut, silk taffeta top and an angora beaded cardigan.

▶ "Beat" looks

As the eponymous heroine of the film *Sabrina*, film actress and perennial style icon Audrey Hepburn spearheaded an elegant version of the "Beat" look, in black back-to-front cardigan, ballet flats and Capri pants.

Novelty themes

Fashion knits, adopted by the teen market, were embellished with "novelty" imagery, such as poodles, cowboys and other Americana motifs, rockabilly themes and futuristic atomic abstracts.

Sweater dress

The undulating curves of the archetypal hourglass figure of the 1950s were emphasized by the figure-hugging character of knitted structures that clung from neck to mid-calf in the popular sweater dresses of the era.

1960s:
Op, Pop and Psychedelia

The first stirrings of teenage rebellion that had surfaced in the previous decade now flourished in the collective desire of youth for change and freedom. All boundaries were crossed and all stereotypes challenged as fashion now became about expressing one's individuality for the teenagers born at the peak of the postwar baby boom in 1947 and who reached puberty in 1960.

The excessive femininity of the previous decade was rejected for an androgynous silhouette that favored the young and slender, epitomized by 1960s icon, Lesley Hornby, known as "Twiggy." The conical bra and the corset disappeared; the stiletto heel was banished; gloves, hats and handbags discarded. All that was needed was a dress or a skinny-rib sweater and jeans, and a girl was good to go.

The 1950s silhouette had gradually loosened since the instigation of Balenciaga's chemise dress in 1958, and the 1960s shift was a natural progression of this line. With cut-away shoulders, the dress skimmed the body and reached new heights. Stockings were no longer an option. Hosiery manufacturers discarded the fully-fashioned machinery required to make stockings and converted their production lines to tights, or pantyhose. Originally made in tubular form and steamed into shape, patterned and textured tights allowed the mini to become micro, and 1966 was designated by fashion journalists as the "Year of the Leg."

The Switched-On Stitch

Fashion was no longer about longevity or quality of materials. In the case of knitwear, it was a matter of style over yarn content. The status of the traditional knitwear manufacturers was threatened, together with their use of noble fibers. Skinny-rib sweaters in one of the newly popular manmade yarns such as Orlon and Acrilan were constructed from ribbed "cut-ups," rendering the expensive and sophisticated fully-fashioned knitwear machines almost obsolete and the expertise of technicians and finishers unnecessary. Manufacturers were challenged by the need for the smaller runs required in a period of accelerating trends. Demand for high-class knitwear in both North America and the United Kingdom fell.

Ironically, knitwear was no longer an adjunct to the fashionable wardrobe, but was now fashionable in its own right. Contemporary designers relished the versatility of knitwear, and used it to showcase Op- and Pop-inspired patterning and multicolored stripes. Futuristic fashions in white and silver of Parisian couturiers André Courrèges and Paco Rabanne were resolutely architectural, but the chain-metal effect utilized by Rabanne was easily replicated by the use of metallic thread, knitted and crocheted into see-through minidresses, and accessorized by the ubiquitous white chisel-toed boots.

The "high" 1960s saw a sudden swerve into nostalgia, as if the scientific advances and the changes in sexual and social mores had been too threatening. The period of retrenchment that followed the metallic geometric shapes associated with the Space Age embraced the aesthetic of the past. In the U.K. clothes from antiques markets such as Kensington and Chelsea and London's Portobello Road were worn alongside bygone military uniforms and the garments of the counterculture. A reappraisal of Art Deco was led by print designer Bernard Nevill, then professor of textiles at the Royal College of Art. The influential film *Bonnie and Clyde* was released in 1967, which consolidated the interest in 1930s fashions and fabrics, not least the ribbed and smocked sweaters worn by Faye Dunaway. Almost overnight the mini became the midi, and remained the new skirt length until the end of the decade.

PAGE 118 Discarding the pretty pastels of the previous decade, this 1966 mock-rib cotton sweater dress features "cut and sew" construction, including a turned-under, cut neck edge and set-in sleeves.

LEFT A tight, long-sleeve chunky-knit sweater with a boatneck and set-in sleeves is teamed with a matching Mod cap. Accessorized at Yellow Fingers Diner in New York City by a Beatle-cut beau sporting a Cabretta leather reefer jacket.

RIGHT Photographed in 1967 by Bert Stern, Twiggy wears a sequined jumpsuit by Gene Shelly of California. Noted for richly jeweled, embroidered and beaded knitwear, including eveningwear, sweaters, suits and day dresses, the designer had thousands of retail outlets in the U.S.

Boutique Fashion

Parisian couture was rendered obsolete by the retail revolution of the boutique movement. This was begun in London by Mary Quant in 1955, by Dorothée Bis in Paris in 1958 and consolidated by Paul Young in New York with the opening of Paraphernalia in 1965. In 1959 Pierre Cardin was expelled from the Chambre Syndicale de la Couture Parisienne for launching a ready-to-wear collection, an indication of the changes to come in the hierarchy of fashion. A young Yves Saint Laurent showed what was to be his final collection for Christian Dior, that bastion of refined haute couture, and shocked the fashion establishment with a Beat collection, featuring black leather, black sweaters and knitted caps. It was only when he started his own ready-to-wear label, Rive Gauche, that he was able to formalize his Left Bank aesthetic. Established in 1962, Rive Gauche later sold through a range of boutiques in Britain and France. Often inspired by what he saw on the streets of London and the avant-garde British designers such as Ossie Clark and Foale & Tuffin, he popularized the trouser suit with Le Smoking, a classic tuxedo for women in 1966.

British fashion and culture were becoming the focus of world attention; in 1963 Diana Vreeland, editor of American *Vogue,* declared "The British are coming." New independent designers such as Mary Quant, John Bates, Foale & Tuffin, Gerald McCann and Barbara Hulanicki of Biba led the world in avant-garde fashion.

Mary Quant designed the archetypal look of the early 1960s – a tight-fitting ribbed sweater and dark tights worn under a short tunic-style pinafore dress in a bonded jersey, which gave an architectural line to the body. She played with the proportions and textures of classic fashion garments; details and unexpected fabrics transformed the ordinary into the special. The cardigan became a coat, stripes were worn with checks and the trench coat was designed in wet-look PVC. Quant was the first designer to dismantle the barriers between day- and eveningwear; no longer was the "occasion dress" the highlight of the catwalk show. The idea of dressing up to go out in the evening was no longer relevant.

In 1961 Mary Quant Limited was formed to manufacture the "Quant Look" in quantity. This was extended in 1963 when she became the founder-director of the Mary Quant Ginger Group. Quant spearheaded British fashion into America when she signed up to design four collections a year for J. C. Penney, owner of one of the biggest chains of stores in the U.S. Fashion entrepreneur Paul Young then initiated "Youthquake," a division of the Puritan Fashion Corporation to manufacture clothes by British designers, including Quant, Foale & Tuffin and Zandra Rhodes. In 1965 he opened Paraphernalia on New York's Madison Avenue, selling European and American designers such as

RIGHT This whimsical figurative design of ranks of happy guardsmen was produced in three-color rib jacquard and used by Mary Quant for flared trousers. The inherent stability of the dense jacquard structure would tend to inhibit fabric deformation in wear.

BELOW Designer Yves Saint Laurent in Paris in 1966 in front of his Rive Gauche boutique. A model wears a closely coordinated outfit comprising a fine-gauge roll-neck sweater with suffused engineered stripes, rising to a solid-shade yoke, and a miniskirt.

THE YEAR OF THE LEG

The year 1966 was designated the Year of the Leg by the popular press, not only because of the brevity of the miniskirt, but also because of the plethora of printed, patterned tights (or "pantyhose") available. As the skirts got shorter, the tights got fancier: pastel "opera hose" (fishnets), diamond and herringbone patterns, printed paisleys and textured ribs, all were the result of the hosiery companies buying modern production machinery that allowed for unprecedented variations, particularly in combination with new and versatile synthetic fibers.

At the beginning of the decade the only hosiery available was "fully-fashioned" stockings. Recognizable by the seam up the back of the leg, these were knitted flat, and shaped by decreasing and increasing the number of stitches creating V-shaped "fashioning" marks with narrow reinforced heel panels outlining the seam at the rear. The introduction of Lycra into nylon improved the elasticity and fit of the stockings, rendering the fashioning process obsolete. By the early 1960s, fully-fashioned stockings were replaced by seamless stockings made on a circular knitting machine.

At the same time, tights were in development. In California Allan Gant manufactured the first "pantyhose," a term derived from "panties" – indicating the opaque section at the top – and "hose" referring to the attached stockings. The British hosiery company Aristoc dropped its manufacture of fully-fashioned stockings and devoted their entire production to tights, producing a "seamless" version. In America the term "pantyhose" is used to distinguish tights of a "lighter" weight or denier; "tights" being the name reserved for the thicker, more opaque garments. In the U.K., the designation "tights" is used as a generic name regardless of weight, texture or denier of the material.

LEFT From Carnaby Street – the epicentre of British "Modishness" in 1966 – a mini-dress in sporty two-color striped cotton jersey by Mary Quant features an exaggerated collar and a signature zip with metal ring-pull. Despite the inherent elasticity of knitted jersey, Quant has shaped the garment with traditional bust darts, suggesting that the designer was yet to appreciate the properties of the fabric.

LEFT The influence of the monochromatic Op Art movement can be seen in these black-and-white dresses dating from 1966. The coarse-gauge mock rib design (near left) by Frank Usher is produced in the synthetic yarn Orlon, and eyelet lace adds texture within the white stripes of the bodice. To contain the drop of the weighty fabric, a ribbon coulisse at the waist anchors and creates fullness. In the "cut and sew" shift by John Bates (far left) the fabric falls straight from the high waist to the hem, while the buttoned placket and collar trim recall the bold, horizontal stripes.

Betsey Johnson. Enormously influenced by Biba, whose shop she had visited while on a visit to London, Johnson was seen as the home-grown talent that could usurp the British stranglehold on the avant-garde.

In menswear, the style revolution was begun by entrepreneur and retailer John Stephen in London's Carnaby Street, then a Soho backwater of run-down shops and warehouses. By 1966 Stephen owned six of the boutiques that lined the street, which became an essential shopping venue for the "Mods," the dominant subculture of the time, who wanted to keep up with increasingly accelerating trends. Traditional male outfitters such as Simpson's of Piccadilly and Jaeger were quick to spot the popularity of Mod fashions, which soon became mainstream. The "designer" tailors such as Tom Gilbey replaced traditional tailoring of Savile Row, discarding the customary interlining and padding in his construction of garments for men. He partnered the suits with the popular multicolored and patterned hand-loomed V-necked sweaters. Men also wore figure-hugging Shetland sweaters in bright colors. Those unwilling to pay designer prices bought children's versions from Marks & Spencer's or boiled up chainstore sweaters to reduce them in size.

Knitwear was one way of mediating the provocative fashions of the times. British designer Jeff Banks, who owned the boutique Clobber, manufactured see-through crocheted dresses so sought-after that he had to ration their delivery to boutiques on London's King's Road. Later in the decade knitwear designer Rosalind Yehuda sold her line of clothes through Woollands 21. Vanessa Denza, the then fashion buyer said, "her knitted clothes are amazing." Sally Tuffin and Marion Foale sold their knitwear and zip-fronted jersey dresses through Countdown, a boutique owned by James Wedge and Pat Booth.

RIGHT Fully-fashioned raglan-sleeved sweater dress by British company John Smedley for the American company Hooper Associates Ltd. Retailers in America preferred close-fitting necklines, such as this "mock turtle," to have a short zip at the back of the neck. William Cotton multi-section knitting frames permitted a maximum of three colors in production, unless the manufacturer was prepared to improvise with interruptions and hand-knotting of additional shades.

ABOVE Carefully engineered in fine merino wool, this fully-fashioned sweater with a "mock turtle" collar was produced in the 1960s for the American company Hooper Associates Ltd. The stripes are immaculately aligned across the body to meet those of the set-in sleeves.

Biba and Barbara Hulanicki

Barbara Hulanicki, who opened her first shop, Biba, in London's Abingdon Road in 1964 with her husband and business partner Stephen Fitz-Simon, provided the archetypal 1960s shopping experience. Hulanicki democratized fashion not only with the affordability of her clothes, but with a groundbreaking mail-order catalogue, designed by John McConnell along the lines of fashion editorials in magazines. The catalogue was shot by innovative fashion photographers including Helmut Newton and Sarah Moon, and the images reflected the implicit sensuality of Hulanicki's designs. Her use of soft wool, cotton jersey and wool crepe were in direct opposition to the architectural Space-Age clothes of other contemporary designers. One of her best-sellers was the granddad vest (called "poorboys" in America), dyed in her singular color palette of maroon, orchid, amethyst, plum and saxe blue, and the Biba T-shirt, with its skinny torso and tight armholes. These were displayed in fast-diminishing piles on the counters of the store.

RIGHT A matching strap-backed halter top and voluminous trousers produced by Biba in the 1960s. The two-color ogee repeat pattern of scalloped fans is realized in fine-gauge rib jersey with "birdseye" backing. In terms of the technology of the era, the scale of the repeat (see detail far right) is generous – elsewhere the mass market used the same machinery to swamp the high street with anonymous, easy-care Crimplene cardigan suits in tiny geometric patterns.

BELOW The sinuous, Art-Deco graphic style synonymous with the Biba label, designed by Tony Little, extended to its expression in the garment forms designed by Barbara Hulaniki, as seen in the dress opposite.

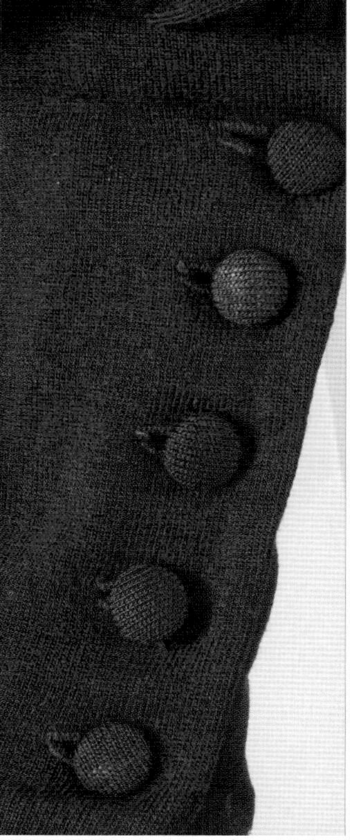

THIS PAGE A Biba "cut and sew" jersey midi-dress flares from the body through the sophistication of the pattern cutting. The fitted effect of the bodice is achieved by concealing the darting in the seam of the dramatic sewn-in stripe across the bodice. Long cuffs with covered buttons (see detail upper left) are used to pull in the exaggerated fullness of the puff sleeves, a trademark of the label.

LEFT Designers Marion Foale (left) and Sally Tuffin in their workroom in September 1965. Sally Tuffin is wearing the best-selling and influential square-yoked dress also worn by 1960s style icon Cathy McGowan, presenter on the weekly British pop-music program *Ready, Steady, Go.*

BELOW In this vivacious 1960s tunic top Marion Foale and Sally Tuffin rework the classic components of a zippered raglan pullover top from an athletics' tracksuit. The transformation of jersey sweatshirt fabric by the use of bright color is teamed with dynamic modifications to the proportion and fit, changing the comfortable and functional to the dashing and modern. In the back-neck label detail it is clear that the traditional methods of tracksuit construction have been maintained.

Marion Foale

Described by *Time* magazine as two of London's "top happeners," designers Marion Foale and Sally Tuffin were instigators of the British cultural and fashion revolution of the 1960s. Post-graduate students of the prestigious fashion course at London's Royal College of Art, they were contemporaries of Gerald McCann (who designed for Bazaar, Harrods, Peter Robinson, as well as Bloomingdale's, Saks and Bergdorf Goodman), Kiki Byrne, photographer Sylvia Ayton, retailer James Wedge and Zandra Rhodes. Foale and Tuffin graduated from the college in 1961 and were among the first young entrepreneurs of the boutique movement to design and manufacture under their own label. They originally sold their clothes to the Woollands 21 shop, a department store which, under the aegis of Martin Moss, was to become a unique retail space selling young avant-garde designers. They then opened their own premises in 1962 in Marlborough Street, just off Carnaby Street.

During the 1970s the partnership ended, and Foale went on to produce her own label knitwear. After spending a year teaching herself to create a properly functioning and accurate pattern, she then designed an understated and classic capsule collection of sweaters and cardigans. When one of her designs was featured as a free pattern in the *Sunday Times* color supplement, demand snowballed, and the sweaters sold in both the U.K. and America. Hand-knit was then an important element in fashion, particularly the "picture sweater" or Fair Isle styles, but Foale's aim was to create timeless designs with the emphasis on perfect detail, stitch and finishing, making garments that reflected her expertise at tailoring and cutting outerwear. In 1985 the designer produced a knitting pattern book and in 1987, Foale opened a shop in Hinde Street, near London's Marylebone High Street.

Marion Foale still creates knitwear fashions today. Manufacturing is done by approximately 300 local hand-knitters and each garment takes 300 hours to make. The designer produces a special three-ply yarn, dyed to her own color palette. Two collections a year are produced and shown at London, Paris and New York Fashion Weeks. The knitwear, inspired by the fit and form of the 1940s, is highly collectable.

ABOVE Film director Woody Allen engages in a low-altitude aerial battle with colorfully clad "dollybirds," wearing, from left to right: a pink chiffon double shift; a paisley chiffon smock; a cross-banded shift in red and acid green by Impact with stockings by Hudson Hosiery; and lastly the jockey-inspired dress by Foale & Tuffin (also as worn by Tuffin, opposite top left).

Art into Fashion

During the 1960s the world of fashion, music, art and film collided in an outburst of popular culture. Artistic movements such as Op and Pop Art infiltrated fashion, graphics and film, removing the boundaries between creative disciplines. Mundane imagery from comic books, packaging, targets and flags, alphabets and numerals appeared on a plethora of products, including printed and knitted fabrics. Hand-knit sweaters displayed the bull's-eye, the Union Jack or the Stars and Stripes, referencing artist Jasper Johns' *Flag* painting (1954–55). In 1965 Yves Saint Laurent fused art and fashion in a collection based on Piet Mondrian's chromatic grids, which he imposed on a simple shift dress of white jersey; subsequently in 1966 the designer produced a range of hand-knitted tunic dresses with geometric-patterned bodies, plain black sleeves and yokes, and a collection of comic-strip Pop-Art dresses.

Ritva Ross

Sweaters were even produced in limited editions as works of art by the knitwear brand Ritva. Owned by former fashion and showroom model Ritva Ross (née Tera) and her husband Mike, the label was initiated in 1966 by the success of a dress patchworked out of crocheted squares. Ross collaborated with artists David Hockney, Allen Jones, Elizabeth Frink and Patrick Hughes to produce a limited edition collection of sweaters of which British magazine *Nova* wrote in November 1971: "Wear it. Frame it. Hang it on the wall. Take it down. Wear it again. Leave it to someone in your will. Sell it for more than you bought it. For it is a very special sweater – a wearable work of art."

Each knitwear design was machine-made from an acrylic yarn with hand-embroidered appliqué, and produced in a limited edition of 150 – the edition number

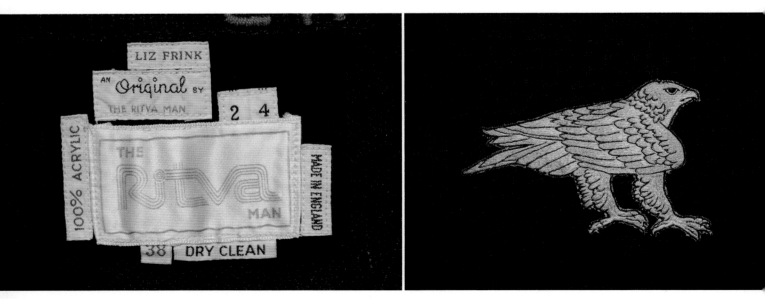

embroidered above the label. Using inexpensive acrylic yarn may have had the advantage of making the garment virtually indestructible.

Ritva Ross was born in Helsinki and moved to London in 1961, where she attended the London School of Printing and Graphic Arts. Her husband, Michael Anthony Ross, was born in Portland, Maine, and educated at Syracuse University. He settled in London in 1960 and studied painting at the Royal College of Art from 1963–64. The couple rented a flat in Chelsea, which doubled as a workroom and showroom, and together they built up a network of outworkers using hand-operated frames. The first designs were ordered by Annacat boutique in South Kensington. Publicized in *Nova* magazine, the line was sold through stores and boutiques in London and the U.S. Customers included Lee Radziwill, sister of Jacqueline Kennedy Onassis, who appeared wearing a Ritva outfit on the cover of *Life* magazine in November 1966. The firm offered a limited number of styles but allowed customers to have garments made up individually in a range of colors and patterns.

In 1969 Mike Ross started the Ritva Man label with sweaters inspired by baseball uniforms. Heavily influenced by popular culture and contemporary art, Ritva introduced innovations such as the knitted mini-dress. A Little Ritva label for childrenswear was also launched and commissions undertaken for the film and music industries. In 1973 Mike Ross opened the Bear Creek General Store at 10 Hollywood Road to sell imported traditional American goods in London. Ritva Ross continued to operate the Ritva export business until 1980.

OPPOSITE In an unlikely diversion from the cerebral character of her three-dimensional work, Liz Frink – later generally referred to as Dame Elizabeth Frink in deference to the international stature of her sculptural accomplishments – makes her contribution to the highly publicized "art on a sweater" initiative by Ritva. Using the simple technology of a hand-operated "domestic" knitting machine, a contrast panel of black low-relief ripples in brick repeat is created in slipstitch. Inside this textured canvas, Frink's embroidered design of a satin-stitch eagle recalls the birds of prey series of sculptures for which she was famed.

LEFT Known for his objectification of the female form, English sculptor and Pop artist Allen Jones, accompanied by a living model, is seen in a gallery showing his work. Both are wearing sweaters designed by Jones for the Ritva Man label, referencing the colors he has used in the painting in the background.

The French Connection

While London was swinging, Paris had its own fashion revolution. From the existential café society of 1950s Paris emerged a fashion aesthetic labelled "Left Bank," a subversive style of dressing in direct opposition to the haute couture of the time. Film stars such as Brigitte Bardot and Catherine Deneuve represented this youthful alternative to formal dressing, appearing in films directed by a new generation of *auteurs*, a group of French filmmakers who formed the New Wave (*Nouvelle Vague*) cinema. Among them was Jean-Luc Godard, whose first feature-length film in 1960, *À Bout de Souffle*, starred Jean-Paul Belmondo and Jean Seberg. Playing a student and an aspiring journalist, who sells the *New York Herald Tribune* on the streets of Paris, Seberg wears the uniform of the Left Bank: the horizontally-striped Breton top that has become a fashion classic, eternally signifying youthful French chic. The striped sweater has continually appeared in the knitwear collections of designers since it was first popularized by Chanel in the 1930s. Chanel's penchant for sailor tops was fuelled by her fascination with the uniform of the British crew working on the Duke of Westminster's yachts. Jean-Paul Gaultier, Agnès B., Sonia Rykiel and Margaret Howell continue to provide a contemporary version of what has become a knitwear staple.

Meanwhile, the Space-Age, futuristic, uncluttered lines of French designers André Courrèges, Pierre Cardin, Paco Rabanne and Emanuel Ungaro demanded a sturdy cloth, generally a tightly woven double-faced fabric that split to form the bonded seams that were an inherent feature of the style (see page 134). However bonded double jersey also leant itself to the precise cut and architectural shapes of the 1960s sweater dress, short in length and minimally decorated.

Dorothée Bis

The original Dorothée boutique was opened in Paris in 1958 by Elie Jacobson, followed in 1962 by the ready-to-wear house Dorothée Bis, in conjunction with Elie's wife, Jacqueline. One of the first boutiques to focus on the youth market, Dorothée Bis was at the forefront of 1960s knitwear design, producing long and skinny maxi-length knitted coats and waistcoats to be worn over minidresses and skirts. During the 1970s, while the hemline rose and fell, Jacobson offered all the alternatives: the mini, the midi and the maxi, all in the same collection.

Dorothée Bis continued to be at the forefront of knitwear design in the early 1970s by espousing the "ethnic" haute hippie look of layered, textured and patterned garments, culminating in the extreme and voluminous layers of 1976–77, in which a typical outfit might consist of a boldly patterned cardigan coat over a belted, striped tunic, over a full gathered skirt, over palazzo-style trousers, with a matching knitted scarf

and hat. This European approach to layered dressing offered a total look and a complete ensemble, including accessories, unlike the American tradition of mix and match. In common with the smoother, more sophisticated silhouette of the 1980s, the company developed a range of knitted dresses. A Dorothée Bis outfit of this period, a navy-and-white striped wool-knit two-piece dress with a deep V-neckline and padded shoulders, was described in a Macy's 1986 advertisement as evidence of "a new body emphasis... curve conscious and deserving of its stripes." During the 1980s, the company created a sports line called Dorotennis, and Christophe Lemaire joined the company as a collaborative designer. Agnès B, the successful French designer and retailer, also designed for the company until 1965.

ABOVE A promotional portrait of actress Jean Seberg, wearing rolled blue jeans and a jersey matelot top. The Breton striped sweater has remained a wardrobe staple, evoking Gallic chic.

RIGHT The innocent abroad: Twiggy projects virginal qualities for French label Dorothée Bis in May 1967. Demure in white, from headband to peep-toe court shoe, the outfit playfully mixes textures, structures and weights – all in one garment, an empire-line mini-dress. The sleeves and dress bodice are hand-knitted in clingy garter stitch, with bands of simple eyelet lace outlining a stripe of fléchage-lace motifs in relief. The flimsy woven mousseline of the cotton skirt is gathered under the cast-on welt of the knitted panel. Textured tights return emphasis to the legs below the floating skirt.

LEFT AND DETAILS BELOW
Epitomizing the 1960s
Space-Age genre, the
graphic profiling of this
jersey tunic dress by Pierre
Cardin is achieved by the
careful assemblage of
contrasting panels.

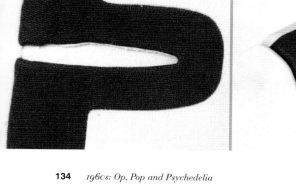

ABOVE A "Jersey Couture"
shift dress by Pierre Cardin.
The black graphic collar
and front band, terminating
in a stylized daisy, cleverly
plays on the female gender
ideogram. There is a further
resonance with more
commercial overtones: the
same daisy was – and is –
a trademark of Mary Quant,
a strong contender with
Cardin, André Courrèges
and John Bates for Mod
supremacy.

TOP The back neck
detail reveals the
endorsement of the fabric
by the International Wool
Secretariat (IWS). The
Woolmark was introduced
in 1964 and the logo was
designed by Francesco
Saroglia of Milan. This
successful global marketing
device acts as a quality
assurance that premium
products only contain pure
new-component material of
a known provenance.

The Beautiful People

As the 1950s drew to an end, Hollywood no longer produced star vehicles for its female actors and the press was forced to look for new icons to represent the fashion industry. Jacqueline Bouvier Kennedy, wife of the young new president, was the forerunner. Accused of excessive spending on European couture, she hired American designer Oleg Cassini, while continuing to buy from her favorite Parisian couturier, Givenchy. The "beautiful people," the socialites and wives of wealthy American power-brokers, felt that only European couture was commensurate with their status. The introduction of the jet plane into passenger service in the 1960s enabled them to fly to Europe to shop and to attend the couture shows in Paris. They were also loyal to the department stores such as Bergdorf Goodman, Ohrbach and Henri Bendel, whose buyers visited Paris twice a year to purchase originals from which to produce line-for-line replicas.

As the "Youthquake" hit America, this status quo was directly challenged by the emergence of a popular culture from across the Atlantic. In Britain the democratization of style was intrinsic to the revolution in music; in America the catalyst was art (bolstered by the relocation of the Modern Art scene from Paris to Manhattan). Dress manufacturer Larry Aldrich sold his collection of Impressionist and Post-Impressionist paintings and purchased work by British artist Bridget Riley and the American abstract painter Richard Anuszkiewicz, and commissioned a range of fabrics inspired by his new acquisitions. The black-and-white optical illusions of Riley's work provided a fertile seam of inspiration for designers and the resulting designs were simple to duplicate for mass-production in both knitted and printed textiles. However, it was not the New York-based designers, but a designer from the West Coast who would provide American fashion with its own iconoclast: Rudi Gernreich.

RIGHT In this reserved two-piece dress by Rudi Gernreich, the body is architecturally sectioned by attenuating vertical panels of three tones of fine double jersey. The dark heavy-ribbed tights reinforce the impression of elegance through drawn-out height.

Rudi Gernreich

Born the son of a hosiery manufacturer in Vienna in 1922, Rudi Gernreich was to become one of the most revolutionary designers of the twentieth century. After fleeing the Nazis in the late 1930s he settled in Los Angeles, becoming an American citizen in 1943.

He studied art at Los Angeles City College and then spent ten years as a modern dancer with the Lester Horton Company, using this early experience as inspiration in liberating the body from the limitations of clothing. His early swimwear designs of 1952 eliminated the complicated boned and underpinned interior construction and the use of Lastex that had been obligatory in the 1950s, and he revived the knitted swimsuit, or maillot, of the 1920s. In her 1967 book *The Beautiful People*, author Marilyn Bender records the response to these garments:

When I showed the first suits to a small group in California, silence greeted them. They were embarrassed. They were used to corseted bodies and those with cones; nobody knew what kind of breasts a woman had. I knew there was a need because well-dressed women had said to me, 'God, I can't find a swimsuit that doesn't have those things in it.'

From knitted swimwear Genreich branched out into knitted tube dresses and then into sportswear. He designed relaxed, comfortable clothes fabricated out of wool, jersey and other malleable materials, usually in solid colors or geometric shapes and checks, experimenting with bold graphics in contrasting hues.

In the early 1960s Gernreich opened a Seventh Avenue showroom in New York, where he showed his popular designs for Harmon knitwear and his own more exclusive line of experimental garments. Throughout the decade he acquired a reputation for being the most radical designer in America. In collaboration with Exquisite Form lingerie company, Gernreich developed the No-Bra bra in 1964, manufactured in a neutral jersey without padding or boning, in which the breasts were allowed to assume their natural shape. His experiments with undress culminated in the topless bathing suit of 1967, modeled by his inspiration and muse, the model Peggy Moffitt.

Gernreich was also responsible for developing the concept of unisex and conceived interchangeable clothes for men and women, such as floor-length kaftans or white knit bell-bottomed trousers and matching black-and-white midriff tops. As the decade progressed, he experimented constantly with the potentials of different materials using cutouts, vinyl and plastic. In 1960 he won the Wool Knit Association award and was given the Coty American Fashion Critics award four times during the decade. Just before his death in 1985, he was given a Council of Fashion Designers of America Special Tribute.

RIGHT AND FAR RIGHT
Rudi Gernreich had a long
association with knitwear
manufacturer Harmon,
who produced his popular
knitwear line. The jacket
here is constructed in wool
rib, trimmed in leather,
but he was also known to
incorporate vinyl and plastic
inserts in his clothing.

OPPOSITE A double-jersey
shift dress in dark rust by
Rudi Gernreich features
darker leather straps, in
various widths, topstitched
in horizontal bands. The
bust darts are strictly
aligned with the geometry
of the leather details and
eccentrically emphasized
by twin-needle overstitch
into a raised welt, as shown
in the detail below right.

LEFT This 1960s zippered
jacket was designed
by Rudi Gernreich. The
attached leather harness
could be seen as prescient
of the subversive impact of
Vivienne Westwood's late
1970s bondage pants. At a
more synchronous level the
streamlining of tight black
knit with leather accents is
redolent of the "Avengers"
style of John Bates'
designs.

The Italian Look

Following the Second World War, Italy underwent reconstruction with the aid of financial support from the U.S., administered through the Marshall Plan, in an attempt to boost post-war trade. This guaranteed that the textile factories of the north had access to capital and raw materials, allowing the small family firms who made up a significant element of the manufacturing sector to continue in business and expand. It then set the stage for the following decade when Milan became the fourth fashion capital, alongside Paris, New York and London.

Legendary designer Emilio Pucci was instrumental in consolidating Italy's burgeoning reputation as a significant fashion center after the war. Born the Marchese Emilio Pucci di Barsento of an aristocratic Florentine family, Pucci lived the life of the athlete as a member of Italy's national ski team. Following wartime service as a fighter pilot, he moved to America, studying first at the University of Georgia and then at Reed College in Portland, Oregon. There he designed ski suits for the Reed College ski team, for which the buyer from Lord & Taylor placed an order. Moving back to Italy and inspired with his first contact with the fashion world, he opened a boutique on the island of Capri to sell his first designs in the 1950s.

In contrast to the constructed elegance and artifice of Parisian couture at this time, Pucci offered a glamorous and elegant alternative that nevertheless required a lean athletic body. In 1960 the designer developed "Emilioform," an elasticated fabric based on a blend of jersey and the synthetic Helanca, which made for a stretchy clinging fit that held its shape. Weighing less than 8 ounces (250 grams), the clothes were portable and required no ironing. The instantly identifiable prints were inspired by Pucci's travels to places such as Bali, South America and Africa, the imagery mediated through psychedelic swirls of a unique color palette. Synonymous with the new "jet age," Pucci's customers were newly mobile style-setters and celebrated beauties such as Jackie Kennedy and Marilyn Monroe.

At this time the Missoni company was firmly established in Milan, debuting their first catwalk collection in 1966. Their fame was assured when, in 1967, they were invited to show at the Pitti Palace in Florence. Unwittingly or otherwise, during the show the fine knitted fabrics became transparent under the lights and caused a sensation (see also pages 166–68).

The Benetton Brand

Distinguished by their groundbreaking and their controversial marketing techniques as much as for their colorful knitwear, Italian company Benetton is now a global fashion brand based in Treviso, Italy. In 1960, Luciano Benetton, then a salesman in Treviso, foresaw a potential market for colorful clothes. He sold a younger brother's bicycle in order to buy his first second-hand knitting machine and produced a small collection of sweaters. These were favorably received in local stores, and soon afterwards he asked his sister and two younger brothers, Gilberto and Carlo, to join him. In 1965, the entity known as the Benetton Group was formed. Then in 1966, the Benettons opened their first store in Belluno, and three years later, another in Paris, with Luciano as chairman, his brother Gilberto in charge of administration, their younger brother Carlo running production and Giuliana as chief designer.

Renowned for the provocative "United Colors" publicity campaigns, photographed by Oliviero Toscani from 1982 to 2000, the company's core business remains their clothing lines. People for the Ethical Treatment of Animals (PETA) launched a boycott campaign against Benetton for buying wool from farmers who practised mulesing (a surgical task that involves the removal of flesh from around the buttocks of a sheep in an attempt to protect it from flystrike). Benetton has since agreed to buy nonmulesed wool and has urged the wool industry to adopt the PETA and Australian Wool Growers Association agreement to end mulesing.

OPPOSITE Emilio Pucci gives this hooded, fine jersey-silk chemise an extravagant polychromatic print, which vibrantly exploits the exotic lexicon of the seasoned traveler. The model is photographed in Udaipur, India, in 1967.

BELOW As early as 1957, publicity material for Missoni declared what was to remain the distinguishing characteristic of the brand: *Due Habiti, Tanti Colori!"* – two dresses but so many colors! In this explosive dress from 1968, the fine-gauge, warp-knitted fabric could scarcely contain more shades, though all are held in order by the anchor of slender black stripes.

Casting On for the Counter-Culture

The burgeoning hippie movement of the late 1960s rendered the singular clean-cut modernism of the early part of the decade irrelevant. Politically the era was marked by a belief in the power of the counter-culture to change the world, and a desire to end the war in Vietnam. Visually, it was an eclectic appropriation of the patterns and motifs of other cultures and a reappraisal of the past.

Hippie culture relocated the youth movement from the fashion capitals of London and New York to the West Coast, where San Francisco was at the hub of the new movement for peace and personal freedom. The desire for self-realization and "doing your own thing" included a rejection of the mass-produced in favor of the original and the idiosyncratic. Personal style was all, whether it was accrued from second-hand shops, hand-crafted, or purloined on the hippie trail that encompassed India and the Far East. A naive playfulness was evident in the imagery that decorated garments: hearts and flowers, fantasy landscapes, butterflies and rainbows. New attitudes to physicality during the 1960s meant that transparency was increasingly acceptable socially, and lace-knitted and crocheted dresses constructed from hand-dyed natural fibers were worn over the naked body.

The effects of hallucinogenic drugs on visual perception were to heighten and distort pattern, fueling the use of kaleidoscopic patterning and vibrant colors in fashion. While this more readily translated into prints, knitwear manufacturers, still supplying the needs of mainstream fashion, certainly began to inject greater color and texture into their products. Flower power was evidenced by the traditional knitwear company Pringle of Scotland's attempts to silk-screen floral images onto knitted garments in 1966. The style fragmentation caused by 1960s youth movement marked the end of the hierarchical fashion system for the next decade, paving the way for the retrospective, the practical and the subversive fashions to come.

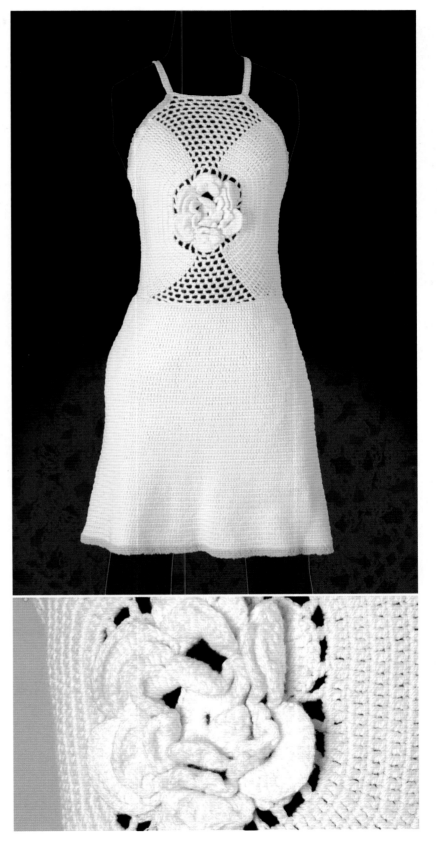

OPPOSITE Julie Christie in 1962, shortly after her first film role in the romantic comedy *The Fast Lady*. Her hand-worked crochet dress in coarse white cotton has a slender line with tight set-in sleeves. The all-over crochet is a loose, open variant on fern stitch, using repeated loop clusters to make a soft handle – and to reduce production time.

RIGHT This white strappy mini-dress is punctuated at hem and top edge with a stripe of lemon treble-stitch crochet. This stitch forms the base fabric of almost the entire garment, with exception of the rosette, which is produced by a floral variation on shell stitch. The lace panels arise from making treble stitch with spaces on a curved path.

◀ Hippie motifs

Flowers, hearts, suns and other hippie imagery embellished clothing. This 1965 bouclé wool pullover by Ilaria Gentucca features an unusually Baroque crochet hem, and an embroidered sun and floral pattern set on a black background. Under the sweater are orange wool jersey stretch pants.

▼ Skinny ribs and sweater dresses

The skinny-rib sweater is elongated to mid-thigh in these machine-knit sweater dresses. Low-slung belts elongate the torso and render the appearance of the skirts even shorter. Over-the-knee socks and tight-fitting bonnets add to the pre-pubescent schoolgirl effect.

Key looks of the decade
1960s

▶ Long cardigans

Chunky long-ribbed cardigans (today popularly called "coatigans") replaced the need for a traditional tailored coat. Worn here with side-fastening woven tweed trousers and a striped sweater, the look eschewed the miniskirt in favor of the longer, leaner silhouette at the end of the decade.

White crochet and knit dresses

The figure-hugging, crochet mini-dress was an essential "dollybird" fashion item, most often in white or ivory with the popular bodystocking worn underneath for modesty.

▲ The "Beat" look

The beat goes on in this outfit by French designer Pierre Cardin in 1969. The black turtleneck sweater and matching tights were the prerequisite for the proto-Beatnik, worn here beneath a futuristic and fetishistic black leather micro-skirt attached to a collar with a white metal strap.

▲ Stripes and psychedelics

Flamboyant shades of hot pink, acid yellow, cyan, mint, orange and mauve caught the explosive energy of a Pop Art canvas. Discordant juxtapositions of polychromatic stripes render this maxi-dress by Ferro a psychedelic swirl of color.

Monochrome patterns

American manufacturer Larry Aldrich commissioned Op-Art fabrics from textile designer Julian Tomchin to make up into clothing, sparking a vogue for monochrome geometrics.

1970s:
Back to Nature

The 1970s are generally dismissed as the decade that style forgot. They were also, however, the period when fashion was in transition, Milan emerged as the fourth fashion capital and American designers began to establish their empires.

The craft revival at the beginning of the decade arose out of the hippies' desire for self-expression. They were inspired by ethnic traditions and techniques culled from the hippie trail to India and the Far East, and an ongoing sympathy with marginalized cultures such as the Native American. Handcrafting was both a means of individualism and a rejection of mass production and the perceived "plastic" values of the 1960s. However, a generation rediscovering the joys of hand-knitting also included the enthusiastic fashion-led knitters, who were inspired by practitioners such as Sasha Kagan, Sarah Dallas, Susan Duckworth, Patricia Roberts and Kaffe Fassett.

The desire to be different also fueled the search for vintage clothes. Edina & Lena sourced vintage Fair Isle before starting their own label producing original pieces from knitwear patterns of the 1930s and 1940s. Biba, now ensconced in the final flagship store in the Art Deco emporium of Derry & Toms promulgated her version of 1930s "Odeon Style" glamour that included sequined knitted skullcaps and matching sweaters and waistcoats.

Scaled-up children's clothes with appliquéd cartoon characters briefly provided a playful element to the decade's fashion mix. In America and Britain the "Ivy League" look had already permeated "Mod" fashion and this "campus style" of elegant coordinated separates became a fashion staple. In contrast to the conservative preppie look, the Punk movement – anti-fashion and visually challenging – ended the decade on a note of subversion that was to pave the way for the avant-garde deconstruction of fashion in the next decade.

For the newly professional woman claiming her place in the workforce, there was no room for fun fashion or provocative punk in the boardroom. For those who declined to wear hotpants, yet refused to shackle themselves in the maxi-skirt, trousers were the solution. Diane von Furstenberg provided a feminine alternative with her iconic "wrap dress," and grown-up glamour for evening was epitomized by the fluid drapery of designers such as Halston and Geoffrey Beene.

Pop-Culture Knits

In 1971 shorts, or "hot pants," with bibs and straps replaced the miniskirt for those women reluctant to relinquish the freedom of the mini for the midi- or maxi-skirt. Tommy Roberts, the British designer and retailer behind the label Mr. Freedom, produced brightly colored shorts with Pop Art motifs of appliquéd lightening strikes and rainbows to be worn with matching multicolored thigh-high knitted striped socks and platform boots and shoes. The "King of Cartoon," Moroccan-born Jean-Charles de Castelbajac, also provided irreverent fashion with knitwear that referenced the cartoon images of childhood. In 1975 he designed a collection for Gilmar wool clothing, an Italian knitwear company established in 1962 by Giuliana Marchini and her husband, Silvano Gerani. In 1978 de Castelbajac created a range of sweaters that featured Felix, Snoopy and Bugs Bunny for the company's Iceberg label, one of the first ranges to propose the idea of fashionable sportswear. Hot pants and comic book clothes had a finite shelf life, and appealed to a fraction of the mass market. Worn with ankle socks, rolled up trousers, and brightly colored leather boots called Kickers, these were children's clothes for grown-ups, in marked contrast to the European elegance that was to follow.

PAGE 144 Designer Giorgio di Sant'Angelo with models wearing entirely knitted outfits from his autumn 1972 collection. The look is relatively contained for a Di Sant'Angelo design, but the imagery he chooses for his long-ribbed, jacquard-patterned sweaters recalls the apprenticeship he won in his teens to study ceramic design for three months with Pablo Picasso. The chunky fully-fashioned cardigan on the left uses a mock rib and textured yarn to keep the soft tailoring in shape.

LEFT Playtime for the grown-ups. An all-in-one playsuit with trompe l'oeil appliqué in the shape of a bow is worn over a skinny-rib striped sweater. Designed by Tommy Roberts for his Mr Freedom label, the model is photographed in the interior of his boutique in London's Kensington High Street in 1970.

ABOVE Kitsch cartoon graphics of Pop-Art origin lent themselves to the free color patterning technique of intarsia knitting. This fully-fashioned ice-cream sweater by Dana Originals sets a tone of juvenile flippancy in the face of tradition.

Sonia Rykiel

At a time when fashionable women were rejecting the rigors of haute couture and seeking clothes that projected a more youthful and modern image, Sonia Rykiel, alongside Emmanuelle Khanh, Yves Saint Laurent and Dorothée Bis, was responsible for the dramatic shift from status dressing to the informality of the Rive Gauche. Born Sonia Flis in Paris, in 1930, the designer married Sam Rykiel in 1953. She was initially inspired to design clothes by her own need for fashionable maternity-wear when pregnant with her first child Nathalie, which were then sold in her husband's shop, Laura, in 1962. With the opening of the first Sonia Rykiel boutique in 1968 on Paris's Left Bank, she spearheaded the boutique movement in her native France.

With her extraordinary mass of red hair and pallor, and her trademark black clothes, the designer typified the look of Left-Bank bohemia. It soon became apparent that Rykiel's strength was as a knitwear designer, transforming a previously middle-aged medium into covetable items for the young. Retailing in New York stores such as Henri Bendel and Bloomingdale's, she was labeled the "Queen of Knitwear" in 1964 by *Women's Wear Daily*.

Her signature silhouette is created by cutting high in the armholes and close to the body, with narrow sleeves, thus elongating the torso. Using a distinctive palette of stripes that are subtle but striking, against a backdrop of black, her designs for knitwear involve innovative detailing such as lock-stitched hems, reversed seams and carefully placed pockets. All her clothes are light-hearted with an element of wit, whether in the use of contrasting textures and shapes, or in the detailing.

In the early 1980s she incorporated text into her clothes, such as "Black Tie" written in studs on a black leather jacket, and the belt of a black lace dress emblazoned with rhinestones that read "Special Edition Evening Dreams." Throughout the 1980s the silhouette became looser, with relaxed tailoring and geometric layers and subtle alterations to a signature look. Sonia Rykiel has become a French institution. Her thirtieth anniversary show in March 1998 was held at the Bibliothèque Nationale de France, and she was the recipient of the Chevalier de la Légion d'Honneur in 1985 from President Mitterrand.

LEFT The support of influential retailer Joan Burnstein of Browns in London was instrumental in bringing European designers such as Sonia Rykiel and Missoni to the attention of the British fashion press and public. Rykiel's informal approach to fashion included the exposed construction of simply achieved pieces and deep colors, usually partnered with black. The long, edge-to-edge cardigan coat in wool bouclé has Rykiel's characteristic bound, scooped, round neck. The weighty fabric gains stability from the interlocking of the bouclé yarn and from the mock 1x1 rib structure.

TOP AND RIGHT Here Barbara Hulanicki references her signature silhouette, with the narrow shoulders and elongated torso, emphasized by the vertical stripes of the main body of the cardigan. The bouclé fabric is treated as a yardage jersey material, using a soft tailoring construction, rather than classic knitwear methods, to attain the geometrical interplay of stripes and button band.

BELOW Low-cut crossover top by Biba, in fine-gauge cotton. The drama of this "cut and sew" garment arises from the bold geometry of diagonals meeting verticals and horizontals, as the dolman sleeves, wrap bodice and deep waist panels intersect.

Hippie De-Luxe

Vernacular dress, where the construction of the garment is rooted in the simplest way of utilizing all the fabric without particular concern for fit, was a source of much inspiration for knitwear designers in the early 1970s. Max Tilke's 1974 book *Costume Patterns and Designs* proved influential in its descriptions of idiomatic clothing from around the world. Knitwear and tapestry designer Kaffe Fassett was one of those who drew on traditional peasant shapes and ethnic patterning for his hand-knits. Born in San Francisco, Fassett studied painting at the Museum of Fine Arts in Boston before moving to London in 1964. Initially painting still-lifes that featured intricately patterned fabrics, it was a visit to Holm Mills in Inverness, accompanied by his friend Bill Gibb, that inspired his knitting activities. Purchasing an array of colored yarns, he learned to knit on the train returning to London.

Vogue Knitting published the first Kaffe Fassett design in 1969: a waistcoat inspired by the textures and colors of Morocco. His understanding and use of color, the manipulation of hues and shades within one garment,

and his ability to convey his enthusiasm to a wide audience made him a significant figure in the revival of interest in hand-knitting during this period. Fassett's persuasive use of color, texture and pattern made him the ideal collaborator with Scottish designer Bill Gibb. He was also consultant to Rowan Yarns of Huddersfield, and published the best-seller *Glorious Knitting* in 1985.

OPPOSITE AND DETAIL BELOW An extravagant exercise in zoomorphism, this hooded cape (opposite page) by Animal Rainbow, the label run by Diane Leslie in London, uses an array of materials and methods to suggest the brooding presence of a hawk at rest. The hand-worked mix of real feathers, flecked Donegal Tweed yarn and fluted satin over-edge serging creates a garment of bohemian theatricality.

BELOW This 1976 cashmere and alpaca intarsia poncho, by British knitwear designer John Angus, makes visual reference to Edmund Dulac's illustrations for *Arabian Nights*, published in 1907. Produced on hand-operated Japanese Jones "domestic" machinery, the shoulder and hem shaping was achieved by the *flêchage* – or holding – technique.

ABOVE Instant vintage in 1974. This tie-front top by John Ashpool for his label Knitting Inc. successfully evokes the charms of an antique, Native American, buckskin garment through a complex array of technical improvisations (also used in the dress on the opposite page). The mottled denim blue of the base fabric is an irregular combination of soft cotton and hard viscose rayon bouclé, over-dyed in the assembled garment and heavily pressed to add drape and glaze to the fabric. The yoke is decorated with hand-intarsia motifs in glossy rayon, while the checkerboard trims and tasseled, color-block, striped body and sleeves are produced on power-operated equipment. The tassels, arising from yarn floats of extreme length, have been cut and allowed to tangle in the dyeing process to add to the unique homespun character and to make the color joins secure.

RIGHT Fine-gauge, intarsia, striped pullover designed by Sue Kemp for John Ashpool's Knitting Inc. label in 1973. Hand-framed in mercerized cotton and grainy rayon bouclé, the striped patterning is matched carefully between the body and sleeves.

The poncho, shawl and kimono also appeared in the knitwear collections of designers such as John Ashpool of Knitting Incorporated. Considered by *Harpers & Queen* magazine to be "the great white hope of the British knitting industry," the designer's initial success was with the Aztec collection in 1973, a range in cashmere and lambswool, and in some models with a grainy inner texture from the addition of a fine rayon bouclé yarn. The intarsia and striped designs, layered into simple shapes, evoked the patterns of South America. Selling mainly to high-end American department stores such as Bloomingdale's and Henri Bendel, his designs appeared in various films such as Woody Allen's New York comedy, *Annie Hall*.

Recognizing the need to develop a more refined aesthetic as the decade progressed, the designer utilized the properties of knitted fabric to form and shape the garment. He extended the ribbed waist to under the arms, and then knitted the body from wrist to wrist, forming deep batwing sleeves that included various intarsia designs, such as a piano keyboard or *trompe l'oeil* flowers. The production was located in the Scottish borders at Berwick-upon-Tweed, and manufactured by half a dozen hand-frame knitters on the Dubied 00 machine. Ashpool did much to regenerate the cashmere knitting industry in the Scottish borders, producing design-led garments rather than the more traditional V- and turtleneck fully-fashioned sweaters of the knitwear manufacturers in nearby Hawick.

The Japanese designer Kenzo Takada's approach to design also included layering and wrapping the body in loose, unstructured garments such as kimono tops and drawstring trousers. His signature juxtaposition of bold, colorful prints mixed with floral intarsia or jacquard knits was prompted by his early days as a student in Paris when he could only afford to buy fabrics from flea markets. As a result, Kenzo had to mix together many bold fabrics to make one garment. His success was confirmed in 1970 with the opening of the boutique Jungle Jap, located in the Galerie Vivienne. The interior was inspired by the painter Henri Rousseau and had the ambience of a tropical rainforest, the perfect background for his dazzling mix-and-match approach to pattern.

Following his success in Paris, fashion entrepreneur Joseph Ettedgui introduced Kenzo to London in 1971, at the same time as starting his own retail career. Later in the decade Kenzo produced his signature striped knits, designed to be worn in layers. He predicted the 1980s silhouette of the upturned triangle and the reemergence of the mini by styling bulky sweaters with short skirts. In 1971 his collection was presented for the first time in New York and Tokyo.

ABOVE Jerry Hall wears a color-and-pattern coordinated ensemble by Kenzo - comprising knitted kimono jacket, hip-belted tunic dress, jersey trousers - all rounded off with arm and legwarmers. From 1976, the look is typical of the swathed and draped knitted contours of the period. The multi-patterned, multi-layers in bold color epitomize the extrovert style of Kenzo Takada, a graduate of Tokyo's Bunka School. Since 1993 the Kenzo brand has been owned by the French luxury goods company LVMH.

ABOVE The Annie Cossins label enjoyed considerable cachet in the 1970s British boutique market for its hand-loomed, patterned knitwear. Using the Fair Isle or punch-card float jacquard technique, this fashioned V-neck sweater has two-pattern colors in each row, in a 24-stitch repeat. Outworkers would use the simple structures available on their single-bed machines to shape all the components of a garment, including trims in "false" rib. In this waisted sweater, the ribby neck binding and cuffs are of plain stocking stitch (with gaps from missing needles), which is then folded double. Good-quality wool yarns gave resilience to this method.

BELOW AND LEFT Kansai Yamamoto was inspired by a variety of native cultures, including that of Japan. He created flamboyant, kimono-inspired, stage clothes for David Bowie on his Aladdin Sane tour. In this cardigan, the cleverly constructed, curved yoke exploits hand-knitting techniques to evoke the geometric designs of Native American textiles in striped two-color Fair Isle structure. The fullness of the sleeve above the cuff is held in check by a long and elastic 1x1 rib.

THIS PAGE Half kimono, half djellaba, this tunic coat with geometric cut and patterning was a fruit of the design collaboration between Bill Gibb and Kaffe Fassett. The combination of low-cut tunic, knee-length tasseled trousers (top right) and scarf were at the core of Gibbs' 1976 Byzantine collection. The cut and shapes owe much to Max Tilke's classic visual history of native dress; the patterning connects directly with motifs from the borders of Turkish carpets and ceramics.

Bill Gibb

Fashion fantasist Bill Gibb was that intrinsically British phenomenon, a designer of great narrative skill, who communicated through the medium of color, print, texture and cut. The romantic spectacle of his clothes connected with the mood and feeling of fashion during a period when historical revivalism and the ephemera of other cultures came together to produce an eclectic aesthetic that could be labeled "hippie deluxe."

Gibb was born in 1943, the oldest of seven children, in rural Aberdeenshire, Scotland. In 1962 he traveled south to London to attend what was then St. Martins School of Art (now Central St. Martins College of Art and Design). He graduated in 1966 and subsequently earned a scholarship at London's Royal College of Art. Henri Bendel was impressed enough with Gibb's work while still at college to buy his first collection.

On graduating Gibb went to work for Baccarat, a label owned by Monty and Clare Black. In 1969 Judy Brittain, editor of *Vogue Knitting* magazine, suggested a collaboration between Gibb and Kaffe Fassett. The subsequent collection was produced by Baccarat and created a deluge of publicity, with the designs featured simultaneously in both American and British *Vogue* and also the British *Sunday Times*. The collection comprised an eclectic mix of patchworked checks, tartans, Fair Isle knits and Liberty print florals, and was photographed by Sarah Moon. Her images summed up the otherworldliness and the romantic, ethereal quality of Gibb's clothes.

Gibb was awarded the British Designer of the Year in 1970, and a dress from that year was nominated as the "dress of the year" by the Fashion Museum of Bath. His 1973 collection included fluid, drapey dresses in Qiana jersey. Gibb entered the ready-to-wear market in 1974 with a commercially successful range of knitwear in collaboration with Kaffe Fassett. Knitwear technician Mildred Boulton interpreted their work on her knitting machine, using up to 20 different colors and threads in one garment. Once orders increased, the garments were made up by knitwear manufacturer Harry Green of Gould's in Leicester, although Boulton continued to work with Gibb, producing bespoke pieces on the hand-knitting machine. The year 1977 saw the tenth anniversary of Gibb's work with a fashion show at London's Royal Albert Hall. That same year he returned to his roots with a collection based on Scottish tartans.

DETAILS CENTER AND LEFT Original sample swatches, dyed and hand-knitted by Fassett, were translated into fine-gauge rib jacquard fabrics with a striped reverse, which were cut and sewn together to produce the zonal geometry of the patterned garments. These fabrics – the two-color jacquard zigzag in black and gold and the three-color jacquard patterned stripe – were produced industrially on automatic, powered machinery with wide needle beds.

The Craft Revival

Hand-knitting was an integral element of the craft revival of the 1970s, which also included printing and dyeing methods, macramé, crochet, patchwork and embroidery. Hand-knitting was frequently featured in the pages of fashion magazines, evidence of the ability of small localized producers to be fashion-led. Scapa Knitwear Ltd. was a cottage industry that began in 1969 when Brian Redding was stormbound in Orkney, on his way to Shetland to buy knitwear for his wife's shop in Antwerp. An introduction to islander Alleen Thomson led to the production of seamless sweaters on the island, with manufacture dependant on home knitters, which reached a global market. An issue of British *Vogue* magazine from the period requests the reader to "forget the old connotations of homespun knitwear":

Homespun, run by Jeanette Hodgson and Brenda Smith in Oswestry, Shropshire, produces knitwear hand-crafted from start to finish: the fleece for each sweater is handspun, hand-coloured with natural vegetable dyes, then hand-knitted by one of the 120 knit-force scattered round the country. Inspired by traditional Fair Isle and Shetland patterns and original 1930s and 1940s knits they make crew- and V-necks… The transformation of a fleece into a sweater takes up to four months. The fleeces are chosen straight from the sheep back by Jeanette and Brenda, favourite breeds being Border Leicester, Jacob, Texel and Shetland Morrit. After the fleece has been spun into yarn, the dyeing process begins. You could mistake the kitchen in the tiny workshop for a witches' cavern. Shelves are lined with a curious array of glass jars containing crushed tree bark – willow, damson, birch and oak–berries of every sort, even dried beetles (better known as cochineal), waiting to be brewed in giant cauldrons.

The wool is treated before and during dyeing with chemicals known as mordants, usually tin, chrome or alum, which with certain dyestuffs determine the final colour. Regular brews contain South American tree barks – logwood for violent blue, Brazil wood for warm coral – juniper berries for honey gold, onion skins and cochineal for hot pink and red, blackberries with chrome for soft sage green.

Patricia Roberts

This desire for the homemade, however, did not necessarily include the homespun, and knitwear designers such as Patricia Roberts were instrumental in elevating hand-knitting to the realms of high fashion. A significant benchmark in this revival was the publication of Patricia Roberts' 1977 book, *Knitting Patterns*, a hardback compilation of her first three paperback titles. These pattern books were unique in that they were styled and photographed with the same production values as fashion spreads, inspiring many of the U.K. hand-knitters of the early 1970s to take up their needles.

Roberts opened her first shop in Knightsbridge in 1976, followed by three more in London and shops in New York and Hong Kong. In 1974 she began the innovative practice of selling knitting kits by mail order, consisting of a pattern and her own brand of hand-knitting yarns in natural fibers and fashion colors required for making up. Specializing in complex designs that include a vast vocabulary of stitches, Roberts continues to design wearable and flattering hand-knitted garments today.

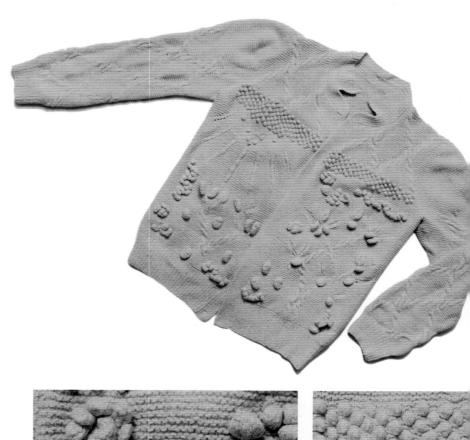

BELOW An essay in pictorial textures, this carefully elaborated cardigan in Arran-style, ecru wool is hand-knitted to a design by Patricia Roberts. The base structure of garter stitch has a diamond trellis of cables, while the front panels use three-dimensional effects such as blackberry stitch, Arran bobbles and garter flaps (see details) to suggest an outdoor utopia of bees and blooms.

RIGHT Maintaining the
irreverence of knitted Pop
Art precedents from the
early 1970s, this Allsorts
hand-knit, pocketed
cardigan by Patricia Roberts
uses a ground of dark aqua
cotton bouclé to support
the scattered confectionery,
rendered in flat intarsia or
in relief color with bobble
and blackberry stitch. The
elevated collar can be
dropped open to form an
angled revere in 1x1 rib.

LEFT Like all toy dogs, Harold has the graphic cuteness that many figurative hand-knits indulged in during the 1970s. Here he guards model Maud in her fluffy, grape-decorated blouson jacket, designed by Patricia Roberts in mohair with blackberry stitch color motifs.

OPPOSITE Two hand-knit sweaters, one inspiration. Patricia Roberts uses the same cherry and grape, Fruit Machine repeat in a V-neck slipover and in a V-neck, three-quarter-length sleeved sweater. The cherry motifs are color intarsia, the grapes in relief rendered in blackberry stitch clusters.

OPPOSITE BELOW LEFT The Pi shawl by Elizabeth Zimmerman was featured on the cover of *The Knitter's Almanac* in 1969. This much-copied round shawl uses a lace-weight yarn; its simple filigree patterns are elaborated with transfer eyelet and *flêchage* lace techniques.

OPPOSITE FAR RIGHT Group shot of Baby Surprise jackets, produced to one pattern, in a variety of spontaneous stripe formulas by various hand-knitters. The photograph is by Meg Swansen for Elizabeth Zimmerman's, *The Opinionated Knitter*.

EZ Knits

A British-born knitter, who eventually migrated to the United States with her husband Arnold Zimmermann, Elizabeth Zimmermann inspired a generation of knitters, including Kaffe Fassett, who learned how to do circular knitting from her instructions. Instrumental in popularizing hand-knitting through a series of books and television appearances, including *Knitting without Tears*, which was published in 1971 and never subsequently out of print, she initiated the Schoolhouse Press in Wisconsin, a mail-order knitting business still based in the schoolhouse and now run by her daughter Meg Swanson.

Though knitting back and forth on rigid straight needles is the norm for most knitters, Zimmermann advocated knitting in the round with flexible circular needles to produce seamless garments and to make it easier to knit intricate patterns. She also supported the Continental, or German, knitting method (where the yarn is held in the left hand), which had fallen out of favor in Britain and America during the Second World War. Continental knitting is preferred by professional hand-knitters, as it is deemed the more efficient method, requiring the shortest number of specific hand-motions per stitch. Zimmermann is credited with knitting the first example of an Aran sweater seen in an American magazine, *Vogue Knitting*, in 1958.

Her "EPS" (Elizabeth's Percentage System) is still widely used by designers: it consists of a mathematical formula to determine how many stitches to cast on for a sweater, given that the sleeves and body are usually proportionate, no matter what yarn or gauge is used. Other patterns and techniques for which she is well known are the so-called Pi Shawl, a circular shawl that Zimmermann claimed was formed by regularly spaced increases based on Pi. Zimmermann is also known for the "i-cord" (or "idiot cord"), and the Baby Surprise Jacket, which is knitted completely flat and then folded, origami-style, to create a shaped jacket that offered a refreshing no-nonsense approach to baby wear.

Painterly Traditions

Craft is a legitimate and compelling way for artists to express an interest in applying their art, and knitting is a particularly accessible process to formulate ideas about color and texture. Both Sasha Kagan and Sarah Duckworth had a background in fine art before becoming proponents of the 1970s craft revival. Sasha Kagan set up her eponymous knitwear company on moving to Wales in 1972. Inspired by the natural world, mediated through the intarsia technique, the designer renders nature into heavily textured knitwear of twisted ribs in natural fibers such as wool, cotton, silk and mohair. Kagan studied to be a painter before going on to study printmaking at London's Royal College of Art. Following graduation she designed costumes for the Black Box Theatre Company until she had an epiphany. As the designer told Karin Strom of *Yarn Market News* in 2007:

I used to buy knits from the 1940s – old Fair Isles mostly – and wear them until they fell apart. One day I had a light-bulb moment: 'I could do my own.' I'd knit and my husband would take a load of sweaters to London to sell. The folks at Browns [an influential London fashion boutique] loved them and bought a few; that started it all. I never plan anything – things seem to happen by a series of serendipitous circumstances. Once I had orders, I put an advert up in the post office for outworkers to help with the knitting.

Two of her pieces are in the permanent collection of the Victoria & Albert Museum, and in 2000, the institute mounted her one-woman show, Country.

Susan Duckworth's experiments with knitting also came out of her background in painting. Enjoying the immediacy and the simplicity of the knitting process she initially worked from traditional patterns, developing stitches found in old books, recoloring, adapting and working out new shapes, preferring simple stitch patterns such as the stocking stitch, which allowed the designer to concentrate on color. More intricate patterns include Swiss-darning, a technique of embroidering pattern into the stitch. After a period of freelance work, Duckworth joined the 401½ Workshop, a diverse group of artists and craftspeople that coincided with the beginning of the knitting revival, when hand-knitted designs attracted overseas buyers. Duckworth's clients included Browns, Whistles and the Beauchamp Place Shop, and other design companies including Dorothée Bis and Gudule.

Sarah Dallas

British knitwear designer Sarah Dallas was at the forefront of the knitwear revival in the 1970s, exhibiting her eponymous label at trade fairs in London, Paris, Milan and New York, and selling her collections to major stores worldwide. The designer continues to work

with the yarn company Rowan, the premiere brand in the sector, producing fashion knitwear designs. This involves color and yarn selection and knitted stitch and fabric development for each product, ensuring that the designs work appropriately and aesthetically within the final range of garments. These are published twice yearly in the *Rowan Magazine*. During the past six years she has authored three books of knitwear designs, and she is currently Senior Tutor in textiles and fashion at the Royal College of Art, London.

ABOVE Getting physical - gym culture and the dance and fitness craze required its own particular uniform. Here a loose, gathered slipover in wool/rayon by Sarah Dallas is worn with matching leg and arm warmers. The prototype would have been produced on a fine-gauge Dubied hand flat, using manual needle selection to create the checkerboard areas of continual pink by holding stitches on one needle bed while the contrast stripe passes behind on the opposite bed. Picot edges – sometimes known as "cat's teeth" in hand-knits – are a recurrent element in the design identity of this London-based knitwear designer. Here she has used them extensively to trim each of the component garments in the outfit. They are created by folding weft-wise strips of stocking stitch that have been perforated by a series of eyelet holes along the fold line.

Adrienne Toth

Producing formal and informal wear, Adrienne Vittadini (née Toth) worked in the tradition of American sportswear designers such as Claire McCardell and Tina Leser. Eager to validate knitwear as a free-standing fashion item, the designer deployed natural fibers to produce easily combined separates of knitted sweater dresses and loose-knit sweaters worn over short skirts or pull-on trousers.

Born in Budapest, Hungary, in 1944, Vittadini immigrated to the U.S. in 1956. Following a period at the Moore College of Art and Design in Philadelphia, from 1962 to 1966, the designer received an academic scholarship to apprentice with Louis Féraud Paris, followed by a stint working for Pucci in Italy. In New York, she designed knits for companies Warnaco and Kimberly, then developed her own line, Avanzara, before starting her own label in 1979. The designer married Gianluigi Vittadini in 1972.

Visual research and a preoccupation with knitting technology were the basis for Vittadini's collections; inspiration came from artists such as Alexander Calder, Pablo Picasso, Joan Miró and Max Bill, as well as Norwegian design and early Russian embroidery. She also tapped into contemporary pop culture for ideas, such as the line she designed based on the cartoon character Dick Tracy. The designer's aesthetic arose out of her engagement with the entire process involved in designing knitwear, from the initial choice of yarn to the finishing of the product.

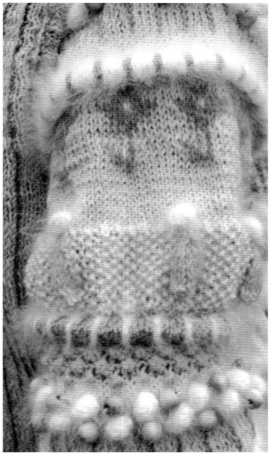

TOP LEFT A detail of a mohair smock with corded ripple-stitch bodice and fluted skirt by Susan Duckworth recalls the textiles and slashed sleeves of the Tudor era.

ABOVE A putty-colored, cropped sweater by Susan Duckworth is hand-knitted in stocking stitch with elaborate three-dimensional patisserie motifs. A raised, lace strap in the arm scye – a further recollection of Tudor dress – is used to anchor the puff sleeve.

LEFT Mock Tudor sleeve detail on a wool-and-angora bolero by Susan Duckworth. Like a historical sampler, the complex pattern is made up of a variety of stitches: cording stitch, Fair Isle, bell stitch on moss stitch and blackberry stitch – as well as beads and bobbles.

ABOVE LEFT An array of gloves and mittens in wool, angora and cotton, designed for hand-knitting by Susan Duckworth. The color patterning in Fair Isle and intarsia is supplemented by three-dimensional components in a palette suggesting the influence of Sonia Delaunay.

LEFT Square-necked, coarse wool tunic by Susan Duckworth. Moss stitch, plain and purl panelling and bobbles are used for distinct areas and for detailing in a stocking-stitch ground. A lacy crochet stitch edges the hem.

ABOVE Knitted gauchos, shorts and short-sleeved cardigan in Glenspun Fair Isle, designed by students at Kingston Polytechnic and modeled outside the Royal Academy, London.

OPPOSITE Edina Ronay and Lena Stengard joined forces in the 1960s, producing their fashionable Edina & Lena hand-knit range. This edge-to-edge, Chinese-style cardigan jacket from 1979 has a face-framing stand-up collar. The bright metallic trim and sharp, satin stitch embroidery with beads moved hand-knitting beyond homely to chic.

Nostalgia

Style commentator Peter York satirized the early 1970s in his 1984 collection of essays, *Modern Times,* as "the Fairisle years," so intrinsic to British culture is the Fair Isle knit and so widespread its continual revival. He cited as examples the television miniseries *Brideshead Revisited*, and the films *Cabaret* and *Chariots of Fire*. He wrote:

> *Fairisle has everything really, it's folk, it's fairly ethnic – like our own Red Indian knitters – it's period, it's provincial or posh. Slap a preservation order on the Fairisles – wherever they might be – give the knitters proper grants, as primitive artists, set up minimum standards and commission a Fairisle tapestry of British post-war triumphs.*

The Fair Isle knitwear stitch was ubiquitous to the early 1970s, for men, women and children. Initially sourced in vintage shops and jumble sales, designers began to exploit its popularity by manufacturing modern versions once the originals had become scarce. As the decade progressed, the influence of the 1930s gave way to the less glamorous 1940s. Sweaters had squared-off shoulders, were shorter in length and round-necked. The tank top underwent a revival and the lacy-knit cardigan was resurrected, particularly by knitwear label Edina & Lena.

Hungarian-born Edina Ronay, of Edina & Lena, trained at St. Martin's School of Art and London's Royal Academy of Dramatic Art. As a model and actress she became interested in antique clothes. Inspired by the knitwear of the previous two decades, she launched her own company producing a range of nostalgic hand-knits, selling them initially from a stall in Antiquarius on London's King's Road. Shortly afterwards, she was joined by Lena Stengard, and by the late 1970s, the firm of Edina & Lena was exporting sweaters worldwide.

Brooklyn-born Ralph Lauren reinvented British country-house style by purloining men's sporting dress, such as tweed hacking jackets, Shetland, Fair Isle and argyle-patterned knitwear juxtaposed with lace-embellished blouses and velvet skirts. In 1974 he designed 1920s-inspired men's suits and sweaters for the cast of Jack Clayton's film of F. Scott Fitzgerald's *The Great Gatsby*. America's own past was plundered in 1977 with his Westerner collections for men and women, which drew on the iconography of the ranch, including shearling waistcoats, fringed buckskin and ankle-length denim skirts. Lauren always insisted the individual clothes were subsumed to the lifestyle, and he offered a compelling and persuasive view of America's heritage. In this way the patterned knit, often emblematically teamed with denim, enabled the urban sophisticate to draw on an aura of open-skied wholesomeness.

The Italian Stitch

American financial support administered through the Marshall Plan of the late 1940s guaranteed the beleaguered textile factories of the Italian north had adequate capital and raw materials to continue production. This economic reconstruction continued through the 1950s and 1960s, and was allied to the long tradition of highly skilled craft communities, which were frequently family-based businesses. This combination fuelled the subsequent success of the Italian fashion and textile industry, and resulted in the emergence of Milan, rather than Florence or Rome, as the showcase for Italian fashion, placing the city on an equal footing with New York and Paris. Whereas Versace established his eponymous label in 1978, providing an overwrought glamour in contrast to Giorgio Armani's exercise in restrained tailoring from 1974, Italian company Missoni single-handedly elevated the status of knitwear in fashion from its artisan connotations to high glamour.

Missoni

Polychromatic warp-knitted stripes are the unmistakable signature of Italian company Missoni. One of the first labels to distance knitwear from its frumpy, artisanal image and place it at the forefront of 1970s fashionable glamour, the label tapped into the latter part of the decade's desire for elegance.

The company was founded by Ottavio "Tai" Missoni and his wife, Rosita Jelmini, in 1953, the year of their marriage. They met in London during the 1948 Olympics: Ottavio, the Italian 400-meter running champion in 1938 and world student champion in Vienna, was a finalist in the 400-meter hurdles. He also had a small firm in Trieste that produced tracksuits. Rosita had fashion experience gained with her family's firm, which produced shawls and linens for the home. They began with a small workshop of three knitting machines in the basement of their home in Gallarate. In 1958 they presented their first collection under the Missoni label in Milan. The business prospered with the support of legendary editor Anna Piaggi, then at the magazine *Arianna*. On a trip to New York, Rosita met the French stylist Emmanuelle Khanh, whose avant-garde aesthetic led to collaboration and a radical new collection for their first catwalk show in 1966.

In 1969, they built the factory at Sumirago, at their home. Then in 1970, Bloomingdale's opened a Missoni concession in their New York headquarters. In 1972, *The New York Times* wrote that Missoni "makes the best knitwear in the world and, according to some people, the most beautiful fashions in the world."

The label's distinctive use of color and texture developed out of a unique virtuosity with the technique of warp-knitting, a process that is a cross between knitting and weaving where a warp of many threads creates vertical chains linked together. The flexibility of this structure was utilized to the full by the Missonis during the 1970s, when the label produced multicolored stripes and zigzags and lightening bolts of color in effervescent space-dyed yarns in their signature flame pattern, inspired by the angular art of the Italian Futurists. Missoni were the first to create constructed knitted jackets, pioneer the use of knitted furs and produce a tweed-effect knitted fabric that had all the substance of woven cloth.

Stitch structure and technical innovation was always allied to the design; Tai Missoni used checked paper to meticulously plan the complex patterns that referenced the basic geometric elements of Cubist painter Fernand Leger and Sonia Delaunay, and the abstract expressionist Paul Klee. He pursued the Bauhaus doctrine that there should be no division between architecture, the fine arts and industrial design, hence the synergy of the label between design and technology and the sources of inspiration.

Towards the mid 1970s, Missoni added furnishing fabrics and household linen to their collections of knitwear, accessories and jewelry. In 1976, the first Missoni boutique was opened in Milan to be followed by retail outlets in Paris, Germany, Japan, the Far East and New York. The creative directorship was passed to the Missoni's daughter Angela in 1997 when Rositta Missoni concentrated on the interiors label.

RIGHT The startling and unique emphasis on combinations of color, pattern and texture, which identifies the Missoni label, is evidenced in this multi-colored tunic top through the use of simple weft knitted stripes. A single yarn traverses an entire bank of needles to make a row of stitches, before a different thread produces subsequent groups of rows in different solid colors. The skirt has zigzag warp stripes in colors, exactly coordinated to the weft-knitted top, using the raschel, warp-knitted fabric rotated through 90 degrees to continue the impact of stratified color.

BELOW A kaleidoscopic patchwork of striped and patterned diamonds are used in this scoop neck, sleeveless Missoni sweater to form the additional visual effect of trompe l'oeil three-dimensionality.

BELOW Characteristic outfits by Missoni. The cardigans are long and straight, using weft-knitted body blanks for "cut and sew" production in a soft tailored construction. The short box-pleated skirt is created on a fine-gauge rib machine. It has a needle "set-out" of a continual 1x1 rib, interrupted at 2-in intervals by single omitted needles – a sequence of two individual omissions from one face followed by two equally spaced omissions from the opposite needle bed.

ABOVE AND TOP DETAIL A Missoni "hostess" dress is warp-knitted in tones of orange, red, brown and mustard.

One-Step Dressing

Fashion in America was evolving to accommodate the modern lifestyle of the urban professional woman. The Women's Liberation Movement demanded fuss-free clothes that reflected their busy lives. The archetypal 1970s silhouette was long and lean, almost asexual; trousers and jackets were cut along masculine lines and close to the body. In 1971 Ralph Lauren, who had made his name with the Polo line for men, produced a line of tailored suits for women, and the polo-player emblem appeared embroidered on the cuff of a tailored women's shirt for the first time. Calvin Klein produced a softer silhouette of luxurious interchangeable tailored separates in classic tones of beige, white, navy and black that were favored throughout the decade. Going to extremes, Rudi Gernreich allied himself to the cause of female liberation by accessorizing his collection for Harmon Knitwear with toy rifles and dog tags.

Devoid of the ragbag accoutrements of hippie culture, designer Diane von Furstenberg invented one-step dressing with the wrap dress in 1972, constructed of a printed knitted jersey of such fine knit as to be almost indistinguishable from closely woven fabric. The dress was integral to the easy-wear, easy-wash, day-to-night fashion solution for the busy working woman. Matte jersey was also the fabric of choice for the best-selling flared knee-length T-shirt dress by Clovis Ruffin. The scoop neck and cap-sleeved dress was equally simple; with no fastenings it was pulled on over the head. Meanwhile, Bonnie Cashin retained her reputation as one of America's chief exponents of separates. In 1972 she founded the Knittery label, specializing in sweaters with a handmade look. A more formal, yet relaxed approach to knitwear was offered by Cuban-born designer Adolfo. Initially designing casual daywear, in 1973 he concentrated on what was to become his signature style: knitted versions of the Chanel suit made in bouclé tweed-effect yarns with cardigan-style jackets decorated in braid and worn with a matching blouse.

The high-end department stores no longer offered a bespoke service and closed their couture departments, substituting a series of in-house boutiques that sold the look of a particular designer, including Geoffrey Beene and Perry Ellis, both of whom consolidated their particular brand of informal ready-to-wear. The ostentatious ballgown was replaced by knee- and floor-length wrapped and backless dresses of Roy Halston, master of the draped silk jersey dress. He championed a fluid silhouette, of which texture was a major component, dressing the celebrity clientele of New York's hotspot Studio 54. In addition to floating kaftans and cashmere ankle-length sweater dresses, the designer added pared-down glamour with ultra-suede shirtdresses and trousers for daywear.

ABOVE The American designer, Diane von Furstenburg, photographed in 1973 wearing one of her iconic, printed jersey, wrap dresses that set the paradigm for easy, one-step dressing.

ABOVE The fabric of this Jean Muir dress is relatively unusual for the label – one of few to use printed jersey.

BELOW A fully-fashioned sweater, with bound Peter Pan collar and keyhole neckline produced by John Smedley in fine-gauge merino wool. The bow is formed from the extended bindings of the keyhole.

RIGHT British designer Jean Muir was renowned for her distinctive use of Hirelle jersey, utilizing the fluidity of the fabric to produce feminine, unrestrictive clothes in which the emphasis lies in the detailing – in this case the top-stitched tie and the smocked waistband and cuffs.

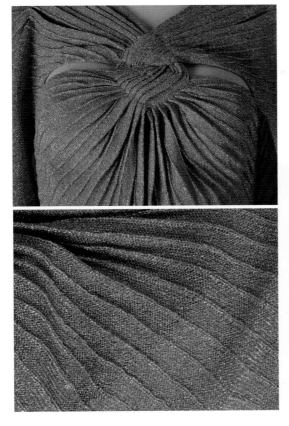

LEFT AND BELOW A gold pleated top, knitted in metallic yarn, is designed by Diane Leslie. The cape-style top with its slotted bodice echoes the Odeon style, recalled in the 1970s era of "disco fever."

BELOW An electric blue, halter-top evening dress dates from 1972 but recalls the decade's revival of 1930s style. It is knitted in metallic yarns with a heavier folded-over rib anchoring the neck strap and top edge binding.

The Preppy Look

Always an important element of mainstream style in America, the preppy look became high fashion and an internationally recognized aesthetic in the late 1970s and 1980s with the endorsement of designers such as Ralph Lauren and Perry Ellis.

Originally the word "preppy," a shortened version of the word preparatory, was used to describe those attending an Ivy League college or other prestigious university, who shared certain characteristics of vocabulary, accent, dress, mannerisms and etiquette. Subsequently, its usage was employed to simply define a particular way of dressing, one that is both understated and very specific in its details and format. Coordinated separates are fundamental to the preppy look, and during the period from 1967 to 1974 these were supplied by Perry Ellis, then working for John Meyer of Norwich, a company founded by Arlene and John Meyer. Ellis promulgated a preppy style with cable-knit sweaters and matching knee socks, kilts and Liberty-print blouses before launching his eponymous label in 1980, where he continued to design innovative knitwear.

Knitwear was an integral part of the preppy look and included elements of sportswear such as the Lacoste polo shirt and rugby shirt. Cashmere and Shetland sweaters in bright pastel colors were popular; for men a button-down Oxford cloth shirt, an Argyle-patterned sweater and cuffed chinos worn with boat shoes were a uniform. In 1972 Ralph Lauren released Polo's famous short-sleeve mesh shirt with the Polo logo. It was produced in 24 colors and soon achieved classic status. Brands that have come to represent the preppy look include Tommy Hilfiger, Jack Wills, Brooks Brothers, Lilly Pulitzer, Gant U.S.A. and J. Crew.

BELOW In the 1970s, John Smedley collaborated with the Byford label. This short-sleeved raglan crew was produced on the 30-gauge knitting frames (with 20 needles per inch) in a navy, white and red stripe.

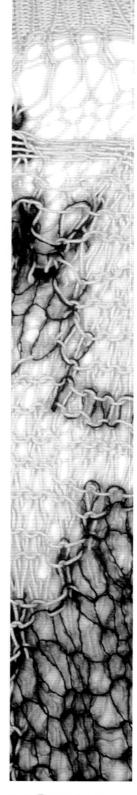

RIGHT The woolly two-tone chaos of Vivienne Westwood's Hangman sweater is an inventive combination of hand-knit intarsia on a laddered plain-stitch base and the integral addition of a tubular-knit tentacle for the noose.

Punk

This stylistically complex decade included the visually confrontational look of the Punk movement, which appeared on the streets of London in the middle of the decade. An anti-fashion movement that was to prove enormously influential, the punk movement customized and deconstructed traditional garments such as the T-shirt by ripping, piercing and printing with subversive images and slogans.

Instigators of this anarchic movement were Vivienne Westwood and Malcolm McLaren, who from 1971 initially sold 1950s retro fashion in their shop, Let It Rock. In 1974 they changed the name to SEX, selling rubber fetishwear and sado-masochistic bondage paraphernalia. SEX evolved into Seditionaries in 1976, providing striped mohair sweaters and fetishistic rubber and leather trousers with bondage straps. This proved a commercial success and secured Westwood's reputation as an iconoclastic designer. Essentially an aesthetic that encouraged self-customization, the punks constructed their own knitwear of string vest-like sweaters knitted on big needles to create large and irregular holes, as worn by Steve Jones of the Sex Pistols on the "Anarchy in the U.K." tour. Westwood subverted the cozy concept of knit with her design of the Hangman's sweater for Seditionaries in 1977. The traditional ribbed collar is extended into a noose and the sleeves are long enough to wrap around the body like a straitjacket. Displacement of uneven stitches to create a chaotic surface with irregular patches of black and white adds to the unsettling qualities of the garment.

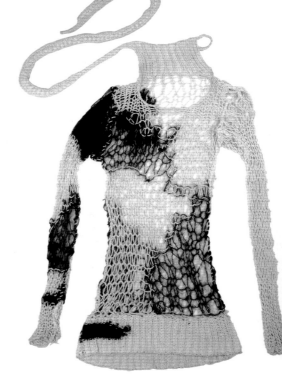

DOMESTIC KNITTING MACHINES

In the 1970s, designers often adopted craft and hand methods to express residual 1960s "alternative culture" aspirations. The implication was that the intervention of the human hand affirmed the individuality of the product. Young designers – finding stagnation in normal employment opportunities as a result of the worldwide Oil Price Crisis – saw the advantages of initially becoming self-employed designer-makers, investing in relatively cheap craft equipment to attain their own "look."

The lexicon of craft techniques that were "reinvented" over the decade can be categorized according to the equipment as well as by the effect produced. Until the 1970s, knitting machines for home use were generally marketed through the back pages of women's magazines; they were engineered as flat-pack replicas of more robust industrial counterparts, with equally limited design possibilities. In Europe they had predominantly been made in Switzerland by Knitmaster, if having just one bed of needles, or by Passap, if capable of rib structures on two opposing needle beds.

Knitmaster began production in Japan, later in competition with other brands such as Brother, Jones, Toyota, Singer and Silver Reed. One of the effects of competition was the generation of rival special features and consequently enhanced versatility. Mechanisms to automate the selection of small-scale repeats were developed – at first a maximum of 8 stitches per repeat and eventually "punch-card" machines settled on a norm of 24 needles, though Passap went as far as creating a cumbersome attachment that took the repeat maximum to 48 stitches. Larger areas of automatic patterning only became possible with the arrival of electronic selection systems early in the 1980s.

Float Jacquard or "Fair Isle" Jacquard: Punch-card machines were a quick way of creating repeated imagery in two-color float jacquard, with designers relying on manual changes in color use, stripes and simple graphics to make a statement.

Weaving-in or Punto Tessuto: Knitmaster offered a special-feature technique for "weaving-in" thick yarns across the width of knitted panels, intended to make skirts less liable to bagging.

Drive Lace: The "drive-lace" feature enabled the creation of panels of thick and thin punch-card patterned lace. In this structure, patterns were realized automatically, with one thin yarn knitting in every stitch in a row and joined in selected stitches by the second, much thicker yarn. The result is that the thin stitches are revealed as the thick yarn floats past unknitted, creating the illusion of patterned transparency.

Transfer Lace: Various machines offered automation of the stitch transfer technique, which doubled up stitches on selected needles and created eyelets when the vacated needle resumed knitting. This was widely exploited as it liberated the knitter from endless repetitions of the hand-transfer procedure. It also made picot edges easier to create.

Intarsia: Like woven tapestry, this technique permitted the introduction of unlimited colors and pattern throughout a knitted panel. Until special accessories became available for the Japanese-manufactured machines, intarsia was only available to expert hand-knitters or to manufacturers who employed highly skilled intarsia knitters using the limited stock of Dubied "00" machines. The domestic machine manufacturers added special intarsia carriages to the armory of accessories. By diffusing the technology to a wider market, derivative intarsia designs were eventually available from most cheap labor areas of the world.

Crochet: This labor-intensive but simple method of engineering garments from continual threads was resurrected in the 1970s. The result had a craft resonance that added an immediate vintage feel to individual garments.

Macramé: From potholders to poncho fringing, the Arabian craft of macramé had a period of intense revival at the beginning of the decade. As well as an association with trimming knitted garments, the technique was used for accessories, such as belts and bags.

Dyeing: As a central issue in establishing the individuality of particular garments, many designers personalized their work by producing a bespoke palette, or in some cases using hand-craft dyeing methods, even incorporating natural dyestuffs. Some designers would engineer colored patterning into their yarns in order to extend the impact of their signature color schemes.

◀ **Hand crochet and knits**
Easily made at home, crochet and knitted garments were part of the back-to-nature crafts revival. Here a crochet "tank top" by Miss Pat of California is worn over an orange ribbed turtleneck sweater in 1971. The brand promoted its mass-market knitwear as "mix-and-match acrylic and nylon adorables."

Key looks of the decade
1970s

Ethnic patterning
Geometrics and tribal motifs, especially those derived from Aztec and Native American influences, were exploited in knitwear patterns and executed in earthy, natural colors by such designers as John Ashpool, Kaffe Fassett, Bill Gibb and Kenzo.

▶ Maxi skirts
The hemline fell dramatically from micro to maxi via midi throughout the decade. British designer John Bates, and sole designer of his company Jean Varon, applied his innovative approach to knitwear in this elegant, fine-gauge matching cardigan, skirt, hat and scarf.

◀ Colorful stripes
A 1970s advertisement for "Knits to Go Nuts About" features fashions sporting "sizzle dazzle" stripes: from far left, a soccer-stripe top; a snug striped sweater and midi cardigan with hot pants; and bib-n-braces and matching sweater.

Ponchos
The knitted poncho, often with a fringed hem, was a fluid alternative to the structured coat or tailored jacket, in keeping with the multilayered, multipatterned, post-hippy propensity of the era.

▶ Sweater suit
A dotted cardigan coat with collar and reveres, cut and sewn in red, white and black jacquard fabric designed by Leo Greer. The bracelet is by Brod; the brown printed velveteen hat by Madcaps and brown leather belt with red suede stripe by Vacher.

1980s:
Subverting the Stitch

The 1980s was an era of conspicuous consumption, one that celebrated success and excess, from the materialistic "yuppie" culture of young upwardly mobile professionals to uber-glamorous supermodels. From 1980 to 1985, the immense strength of the American dollar meant that there was a new clientele for haute couture: Karl Lagerfeld rejuvenated the house of Chanel and a new couture house was established by Christian Lacroix in 1987; fashion empires were also created by Ralph Lauren and Calvin Klein in America, and in Italy by Gianni Versace and Giorgio Armani.

Knitwear provided a stylistic contrast to the power dressing of the 1980s "glamazon," as she "dressed for success" in her stilettos and padded shoulders. Tailoring achieved an importance not seen in fashion since the 1930s, exemplified by the masculine silhouette deployed by Calvin Klein and Ralph Lauren, whose clothes for Diane Keaton in her role as Annie Hall in Woody Allen's 1930 film were particularly influential. As the decade progressed, the shoulder pad reached epic proportions in TV soaps such as *Dynasty* and it was possible to buy them in detachable form with a Velcro strip to provide the requisite silhouette.

Daywear was cut on generous lines with wide-shouldered mid-calf shirtdresses, and the new urban leisurewear included oversize slash-necked T-shirts, often with a vibrant print. British designer Katharine Hamnett featured political slogans, including a demand for a "Worldwide Nuclear Ban Now" and "Stay Alive in '85" for the anti-heroin campaign. These were worn over the ubiquitous leggings or stretch miniskirt. Designer, retailer and entrepreneur Joseph Ettedgui offered the oversize picture sweater alongside the body-conscious stretch knits of "King of Cling," Azzedine Alaïa. John Galliano applied his whimsical romanticism to cream hand-knitted short cotton cardigans for Ettedgui's knitwear line, Joseph Tricot. He attached delicate knitted lace collars to extra-long sleeves with cropped bodices, worn with fine cotton, voile ribbon-threaded dresses. Other British designers, such as Bodymap, rendered London the hub of wild and iconoclastic ideas with their mix of highly patterned print and knitted garments.

Day to Evening

American designer Donna Karan offered a softer, yet still disciplined alternative to the hard-edged tailoring required by power dressing. She exemplified the desires of the aspirational working woman with her wearable capsule wardrobe, which included the "body," an all-in-one knitted jersey sweater featuring snaps between the legs to prevent it from riding up with wear. This was worn under the much-copied jersey sarong skirt and, with matte black opaque tights, became the working uniform for the female urban professional. A promotional video for the designer shows a contemporary New Yorker in the back of her chauffeur-driven car on the way to the office. Reflected in her sunglasses are the city skyscrapers. The voice-over murmurs, "I live for luxury, for the real things. A little cashmere… something soft against my skin."

Knitwear achieved a luxurious look: noble fibers such as cashmere and vicuna were structured into thickly textured oversize cardigans by Italian companies such as Umberto Ginocchietti and Missoni, who now included menswear in their lines. For women the contemporary silhouette of the upturned triangle included the batwing sleeve, providing swathes of material across the torso that were often decorated with appliquéd motifs or intarsia patterns within the knitted structure. The use of natural colors, such as beige, cream, black and navy, gave way to fuchsia pink and electric blue, often configured into startling large-scale geometric patterns teamed with black.

Eveningwear had never been more sumptuous. Jewel colored duchesse satin, silk, velvet and cashmere were utilized by designers such as Oscar de la Renta for the occasion dress, which got plenty of outings in an America newly in thrall to the formal ball and dinner of the Reagan administration. Sweaters were bejeweled, beaded and overprinted – and extended to the ground for evening. Ralph Lauren produced long tubes of beaded, body-skimming Argyle check cashmere while Bill Blass designed a long-line twinset in cashmere that buttoned down the back from a low "V" to be worn with ankle-length silk taffeta skirts. German label Escada provided the "power knit." Exuberantly colored, with strong graphic images, it was the knitwear choice for the career woman once she had escaped the office.

PAGE 176 The archetypal 1980s silhouette from Sonia Rykiel: the upturned triangle, with batwing sleeves upheld by squared-off shoulder pads and narrow skirt or trousers.

BELOW Relinquishing connotations of 1940s utilitarian headgear, the knitted turban was made popular by Joan Collins in the soap opera *Dynasty*. This beaded version is by Italian couturier Valentino and matches the deep-ribbed cuffs, embroidered with silver sequins, of the black crew-neck cashmere sweater with batwing sleeves.

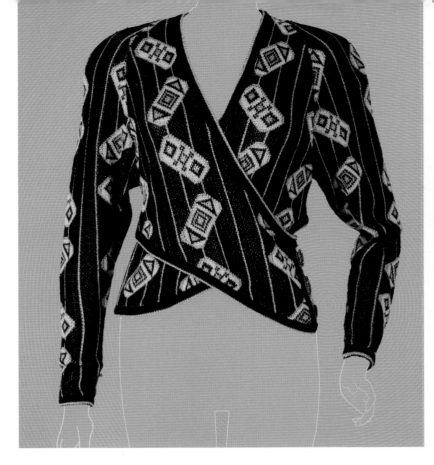

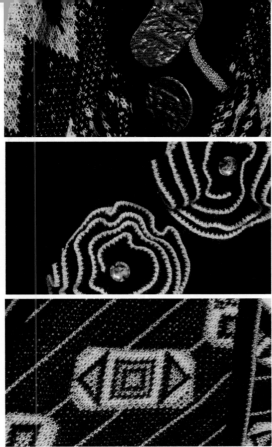

ABOVE AND DETAILS TOP AND BOTTOM Zandra Rhodes is primarily a textile designer, and produced garments inspired by ethnic clothing that reflected her interest in indigenous pattern. Here the simple wrap-around cardigan with raglan sleeves in viscose, acrylic and metallic yarns features motifs from Pre-Columbian art. The fine-gauge fabric is a three-color birdseye-backed jacquard jersey, produced as yardage for "cut and sew" manufacture.

BELOW LEFT AND DETAIL ABOVE CENTER An angora-and-wool-mix cardigan with tie front by Sonia Rykiel is embellished with appliquéd rosettes. The spiral of the petals is created from a shallow band of 1x1 rib with a fine welt stripe of white, in a perpendicular coil buttoned to the base fabric.

The Big Picture

Certain designers have always engaged in narrative, deploying visual research to provide compelling images in contrast to those who are more preoccupied with ideas, shape or structure. The outsize sweater provided the perfect canvas for playfully deconstructed historical motifs, classical statues and antique architectural details, medieval tapestries and the galloping horses that frequently decorated 1980s knitwear. British designer Martin Kidman produced a range of these graphic, hand-knitted sweaters for the Joseph Tricot label. The garments were made up by a group of outworkers under the direction of the Nancy Vale Company, who provided this service to a number of designers. Relatively simple to execute in stocking stitch and intarsia, the sweaters were much-copied by hand-knitters. The oversize garments were worn with leggings or the long, narrow stretchy rib skirts made popular by French designer, Jean-Paul Gaultier.

Following Kidman's degree in knitwear design from the University of Brighton, the designer studied for a master's degree at St. Martins College of Art and Design, where Joseph Ettedgui immediately recruited him on sight of his graduation show. Kidman went on to become design director of Joseph Tricot before launching his own label in 1995. Moving away from the chunky hand-knit, his designs were manufactured in a unit in the Scottish Borders utilizing industrial fully-fashioned machines and the electronic computer-driven Shima Seiki machine.

Other designers engaged with the big picture: British designer Bernie Yates added Swiss-darned figures to her sweaters, and before James and Jessie Seaton began Toast, their thriving mail-order business, the couple produced a range of chunky knits replicating medieval tapestries that sold to American department stores and Browns in London.

Italian label Krizia also featured large, graphic images. An animal menagerie parade across the designer's knitwear, which was shaped into a more sensuous and elegant silhouette as the decade progressed. The label continues to combine a certain mannered excess, expressed in bold colors and luxurious textures with the Italian predilection for animal print. Krizia's official debut occurred in 1957 at the Samia in Turin, although the founder of the label, Mariuccia Mandelli, had already produced a range of outerwear from a small Milan workshop. In 1967 the designer's passion for knitwear prompted her to launch Krizia Maglia – this was the year when she met Aldo Pinto, who would become her husband and working partner. Using the intarsia technique, the designer's industrial knitwear features sheep, cats, bears, foxes, leopards and tigers – a stylized predatory panther is the symbol of the label.

In 1964 Krizia showed her collection of black-and-white plissé dresses worn with mini cardigans at Florence's Palazzo Pitti and was awarded the Critica della Moda. Handcrafting soon proved impractical and the company began to manufacture garments industrially in a factory on the outskirts of Milan. With Walter Albini (who produced knitwear under the Callaghan brand) and Missoni, the Krizia label was among the first to leave Florence for Milan, where Mandelli had presented her models since the early 1970s. In 1984, she opened her business headquarters in the historical Palazzo Melzi d'Eril in via Manin.

BELOW Oversized sweaters featuring large-scale images of exotic animals were the signature style of Italian fashion house, Krizia. An entire menagerie has been created over many seasons, in this case for spring/summer 1980. In the heavier autumn/winter collections, the base image was created on hand-intarsia machines. The fabric was then further embellished with various embroidery techniques as appropriate: beading, glossy satin stitch, Swiss-darning, and so on. Throughout the history of the Krizia label, the designers have felt an obligation to include token animal portraits in their collections.

Escada

During the late 1970s manufacturers began to appreciate the added cachet accruing to the designer label and the selling power of the logo. Escada was founded in the early 1970s by husband-and-wife team Wolfgang and Margaretha Ley as a knitwear company in Munich, Germany. In 1979 the Leys decided to join the designer trend and establish their own brand name. For this, the company chose the name Escada, after a racehorse in Ireland. The Escada label was soon established as a brand leader of Germany's high-end fashion and knitwear industry alongside Hugo Boss, Jil Sander, Joop! and Mondi.

Swedish-born Margaretha Ley had already established a successful career as a runway model for the Parisian designer Jacques Fath in the 1960s, prior to which she worked for Sweden's royal tailor Leja, where she gained experience in designing and producing clothing. In the late 1960s and early 1970s, Ley also worked as a designer for the German clothing firm, Mondi. She married entrepreneur Wolfgang Ley in 1974 and together they launched the contract knitwear business in 1976, with Wolfgang Ley in charge of the financial, administrative and manufacturing side of the business while Margaretha Ley established the company's reputation for design and color, the result of her Swedish heritage. Immediately commercially successful, Escada went on to introduce the Laurel label, featuring designs that targeted the mid-price sector. The Laurel label was also successful, outselling the Escada brand by a number of pieces.

Escada remained the group's flagship, the high-priced line fulfilling the needs of the working woman with a substantial income of her own. During the 1980s, Escada enjoyed rapid expansion, aided by the launch of its own chain of retail stores in Europe's major cities, as well as New York and Japan. The company's entry into the U.S. occurred in 1981, accounting for 21 percent of the group's sales. In 1986, Escada went public, listing its stock on the Frankfurt Stock Exchange – the Leys nonetheless retained 76 percent of the common stock (later reduced to 51 percent). Among other acquisitions, the company also included its first licenced brand, Cerruti 1881, produced under license from Cerruti starting in 1988, and the Crisca, Apriori and Natalie Acatrini labels. Escada's knitwear segment grew significantly in 1989 when the company reached an agreement to acquire 80 percent of California-based St. John Knits. Like Escada, St. John was a family-controlled company targeting the high-end and luxury sectors. The acquisition not only gave Escada a manufacturing presence in the United States, it also boosted its presence in major department stores such as Neiman Marcus, Nordstrom and Saks Fifth Avenue.

BELOW AND DETAILS Strong primary colors teamed with black were a feature of the power sweaters designed by Margaretha Ley of German label Escada. The stylized images, which have been created by the free-patterning technique of hand-machine intarsia, are directly derived from the paintings of Franz Marc of the Blaue Reiter group of artists from the beginning of the twentieth century.

Joseph Tricot

Moroccan-born Joseph Ettedgui was instrumental in placing knitwear within the context of high fashion during a period preoccupied with power dressing. His support for innovative designers and his unique point of view made him the most successful and influential retailer of the decade. He shaped not only the British taste in fashion, but was also instrumental in popularizing the stark monochrome and minimalist interior and the use of industrial materials in both the retail environment and the domestic interior. Ettedgui arrived in London in 1969 and opened a tiny clothes shop called Coco in the Antiquarius market on the King's Road. Expansion relocated him first to South Molton Street and subsequently Sloane Street, where the store's interior by British architect Norman Foster set a benchmark for industrial styling.

With a retail empire of 19 London stores by the mid 1980s, including Joseph Pour La Maison and Joe's Cafe on London's Sloane Street, designed by Czech architect Eva Jiricna, Ettedgui provided a blueprint for a lifestyle. After introducing Japanese designer Takada Kenzo's multipatterned knits to London in the 1970s, Ettedgui continued to showcase the work of young and untried designers, including Katharine Hamnett, Franco Moschino, John Galliano, Bodymap and Azzedine Alaïa.

In 1977 Ettedgui introduced the Joseph Tricot line to run parallel with his eponymous label of sophisticated urban daywear. The collection comprised heavily textured ribbed sweaters to be worn with knitted leggings, tubular, ankle-length, rib-knit skirts and strikingly patterned cardigans, as well as wrap tops and fine jersey T-shirts in neutral tones. One of the designer's basic perennial designs was a chunky cream cardigan with gold buttons, boldly decorated in black, which first appeared in 1987. Known for the superb quality of his knits, he was awarded knitwear designer of the year in 1990, 1992, 1993 and 1994 for his Tricot collection; he died in March 2010.

The Advent of the Designer–Manufacturer

The decade saw the relatively new phenomenon of the designer/manufacturer producing work from their own craft-based studio. Having despaired of an industry fearful of innovation and the avant-garde, designers began to explore new ways of manufacturing, distributing and marketing their own products. For British company Bodymap this was done through the idea of the fashion show as performance art with a catchy title, which explained the concept of the collection in a diverting and witty way. Set up by Stevie Stewart and David Holah in 1982, former graduates of Middlesex College of Art, Bodymap's first collection, titled Olive Oyl, displayed their signature use of different thicknesses of jersey together with jacquard knits and knitted velor in a collection referencing their irreverent use of traditional knitting techniques.

Bodymap's most famous show was held in 1984 and entitled "Cat in a Hat takes a Rumble with a Techno Fish." A combination of separates, the range included woven and knitted fabrics in black and white and featured the striking graphic geometric prints of textile designer Hilde Smith, which were printed on fine cotton/Lycra blend jersey. The legging design included the much-copied keyhole pockets. Innovative seaming featured the one-seamed fishtail skirt, which was knitted sideways on a manual machine using the short-row technique. Displaced seams alternatively concealed and revealed the body in movement. The label produced a total look: leggings, socks, shirts, dresses, knitwear and belts were all part of the collection.

Maria Cornejo and John Richmond of design label 3D (Destroy, Disorder and Disorientate) introduced a tougher edge to knitwear with their range for Joseph Tricot. Playing with notions of gender and juxtaposing contrasting fabrics, the design duo added assertive details such as metal zips and pins to a traditionally soft medium. Artwork was set up in 1978 by Jane and

THIS PAGE Bodymap used radical adjustments to proportion to startling effect. Setting aside the contrasting addition of lacy red bobble stitch inserts, this chunky hand-knit crop top, below, owes much to the traditional Guernsey sweater. However, with distortion of the double-width hem it forms a strong graphic form, teamed with the verticality of the tight tube skirt, right.

RIGHT Crochetta London Ltd., owned and run by husband-and-wife team, Leah and Jonathan Hertz, was a leading knitwear manufacturer during the 1970s and 1980s. In this piece, the cotton yarn has been dyed with indigo before being knitted into panels running transversely across the garment. The base fabric has then been spattered with a bleaching agent to create a milky way of white spots, with bright stellar bodies highlighted with sequins and framed in bold appliqué forms in woven denim.

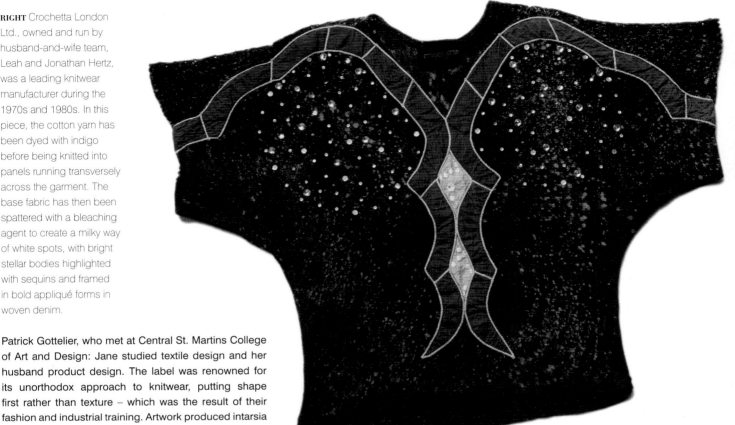

Patrick Gottelier, who met at Central St. Martins College of Art and Design: Jane studied textile design and her husband product design. The label was renowned for its unorthodox approach to knitwear, putting shape first rather than texture – which was the result of their fashion and industrial training. Artwork produced intarsia knitwear overprinted with cherubs and motifs from Greek and Roman antiquity, which reflected the current interest in classical design. However, the duo was renowned for their denim-effect garments produced in 1984, which deployed indigo-dyed cotton yarn that faded with washing. This line was considered highly desirable, especially in the chunky, square-shaped interpretation of a denim jacket. Nearly 30 years on, Artwork is a fashion brand with its main markets in the U.S., Japan and Italy. Today, it designs and manufactures not just knitwear but also ranges of clothing for men, women and children.

Kay Cosserat enjoyed a more organic and less graphic approach to knitwear. Although she designed for many of the leading brands of the era, from Donna Karan to Calvin Klein, her eponymous label featured a soft, loose silhouette in subtle hues of contrasting textured yarns. Technically expert, Cosserat graduated with first-class honors in art and design from Goldsmiths, London, before studying for an M.A. in textiles at the Royal College of Art. She established her label with Christopher Cosserat, a fellow R.C.A. student whom she married in her graduation year. This enterprise developed into the Cosserat Design Partnership in 1974, the same year that she was instrumental in the formation of the London Designer Collections, the precursor to London Fashion Week, which showcased and sold the work of British fashion designers. Cosserat was also a visiting professor at the London Institute and an influential and inspirational lecturer. In 1986 she was elected by the Royal Society of Arts as a Royal Designer for Industry.

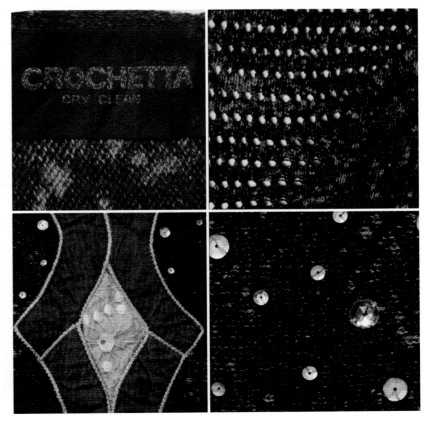

American Casual

Throughout the 1980s the preppy style continued to be a significant element of American fashion. The look had now spread off-campus to become a "dress down," off-duty uniform for the yuppies of the era. Although informal, preppy was by no means laidback and certain rules about particular brands and types of accessory had to be rigidly adhered to. Classic knitwear was intrinsic to the look and pastel colored twinsets always deemed appropriate. Pink and pale green were the most poplar colors for sweaters, often worked into the Argyle pattern, worn over cotton print blouses or the polo shirt in jersey knit cotton piqué (originally labeled the tennis or golf shirt).

Preppy style was espoused by the brand J. Crew. Founded as Popular Merchandise by Mitchell Cinader and Saul Charles, J. Crew launched in 1983 with the mailing of its first catalog. Six years later, the company opened a flagship store at New York's South Street Seaport. Today, the business includes retail and outlet stores nationwide and an ever-growing online and catalog business.

Upmarket casual dressing was provided by Ralph Lauren, whose vision encompassed a world nostalgic for a more leisured, more measured past, one that included English country-house pursuits such as croquet and boating on the river, safari expeditions in Kenya and shooting on Scottish estates. Knitwear was an essential component of these collections, valued for its heritage and craftsmanship. These virtues are evident in Lauren's

interpretation of old classics: prairie knits worn with denim, cream cashmere cardigans teamed with tennis whites and the navy-and-white striped sailor's *maillot*. In 1980 Lauren produced the Sante Fe collection, a glorious evocation of the colors, textures and patterns of the Navajo Indians. The richly colored and elaborately patterned chunky sweaters, accessorized by silver belts, petticoats and blanket jackets, proved enormously influential on the mass market.

Chanel's simple two-piece suit of boxy jacket and narrow knee-length skirt remained a staple of the 1980s' wardrobe. Adolfo, a favorite of Nancy Reagan, the President's wife, and leader of America's "shiny set," continued to produce subtle, understated cardigan suits with discreet trimmings. He also designed simply shaped chemise dresses in knitted bouclé with batwing sleeves patterned in brightly colored geometric designs.

Dutch-born designer Koos van den Akker also produced appliqué-edged two-piece cardigan suits, although he is probably best remembered – in knitwear terms – for the sweaters that he designed for actor Bill Cosby, whose appearance in the eponymous long-running and popular TV series, *The Cosby Show*, showcased van den Akker's multipatterned and colorful knits. The designer produced both a ready-to-wear and a couture line from his boutique on New York's Madison Avenue that collaged, appliquéd and quilted knitwear into abstract patterns.

INSET TOP Short-sleeved sweater in Sea Island cotton was produced by John Smedley for the Jasper Conran label in the 1980s. The designer has subtly differentiated his version of the fully-fashioned polo from the standard Smedley shape by lengthening the button band and the depth of the waist rib, gathering the fullness of the bodice.

INSET BOTTOM Smedley manufactured this Argyle-check women's sweater on behalf of British luxury goods label, Aquascutum. The V-neck style – named Lloyd - was produced automatically on a 21-gauge (14 needles per inch) Schoeller intarsia full-fashioning frame.

OPPOSITE A geometrically-patterned women's turtleneck in merino wool by John Smedley for the American label Bleyle. The garment was produced on a Schoeller full-fashioning frame that allowed the production of multicolored intarsia patterns that generally – compared to hand production – had a vertical emphasis.

LEFT In contrast to the "glamazon" fashion of the era, Ralph Lauren concentrated on his understated British-American heritage look, evidenced here by a taupe cable and popcorn stitch hand-knit Aran sweater worn over a blouse with antique lace collar and cuffs. The striped skirt is knitted in a traditional Fair Isle pattern.

LEFT AND DETAILS RIGHT
Body armor: exposed zips,
emphasized by double
rows of contrasting top-
stitching, circle the body
in this cleverly constructed
jersey carapace by
Azzedine Alaïa.

Body-Con Fashion

The 1980s body was honed and toned to perfection in a culture that prescribed self-improvement for all physical, personal or professional failings. The relentless work involved in honing and toning the body to physical perfection demanded recognition and this came in the form of body-conscious dressing from designers such as Azzedine Alaïa and Stephen Sprouse. Favorite of the supermodels, Tunisian designer Alaïa constructed clothes along the same principles as corset-making, utilizing the property of the fabric to mold the body beneath the dress. Prior to his success in the 1980s, he studied sculpture at the Beaux Arts in Tunis before coming to Paris in the 1950s, when he had a brief apprenticeship at Christian Dior followed by two seasons at couture house Guy Laroche, where he honed his tailoring skills.

Dubbed "King of Cling" by the 1980s fashion press, Alaïa was instrumental in putting stretch, including the short, tubular miniskirt and bodysuit, into mainstream fashion. Influenced by Madeleine Vionnet, the master cutter from the 1920s, Alaïa also worked directly onto the body to achieve the perfect fit: combined with the use of elasticated fabrics, this resulted in garments that created an hourglass silhouette. Although his clothes appear to follow the line of the body, they actually create their own shape, inventing curves where there are none and flattening those not required. Alaïa introduced his first ready-to-wear collection of body-conscious clothes in 1980 and continued to work privately for individual customers until the mid-1980s.

The signature Alaïa look began to emerge in 1985 with the iconic side-laced dress and the long-sleeved scoop-neck dress accessorized with matching opaque tights and shoes appeared in 1987. These were invariably styled with slicked-back hair and red lipstick to produce a streamlined, overtly sexy silhouette at odds with the loose, oversized clothes of the earlier part of the decade.

Alaïa favored jacquard knitted stretch fabric, which he applied to dresses, leggings and bodysuits, but he continually experimented with fabrics, including a velvet-like speciality viscose chenille yarn that produced a fabric with the density of woven cloth, while remaining pliable. In 1994, he showed long dresses in houpette, a stretchy new fabric that molded to the body. The following year he made clothes out of Relax, an antistress fabric with carbon-dipped fibers that repelled electromagnetic waves.

Global labels and big brands exploited the desire for physical perfection as sports became commercialized during the 1980s. Jane Fonda built an aerobics empire by instructing women to "feel the burn," while movies such as *Flashdance* in 1983 and Alan Parker's *Fame* in 1980 convinced them of the need for physical fitness and showcased the clothes in which to achieve this. Nike, Adidas and Reebok were all worn on the street and though not yet considered fashion items, the tracksuits influenced the designs of Norma Kamali, who introduced sportswear into mainstream fashion with her collection of short pull-on skirts, leggings, crop tops and jumpsuits entirely based on gray, fleece sweatshirt material.

Born in New York, Kamali studied fashion illustration at the Fashion Institute of Technology in her native city and graduated in 1964. In 1986, the designer opened the first of her stores selling the "mod" fashions that she had seen on her trips to London. Encouraged by its success, Kamali started her own clothing line and expanded to Madison Avenue in New York City in 1974.

BELOW Azzedine Alaïa photographed in 1985 with the model Farida. Form-fitting fashion combined power-dressing with intimations of the dominatrix. The look relied on a severe silhouette, which included opaque black tights, still a fashion staple.

The designer is credited with inventing many innovative designs, including the quilted sleeping-bag coat in 1975, a collection of styles created from actual silk parachutes, high-heeled sneakers and the popular packable, multiuse poly-jersey clothing that can be worn in a variety of ways.

In 1978 Kamali divorced her husband, opened a new store at 6 West 56th Street in New York City and started her OMO (On My Own) line of clothing. Around this time, she created her famous sweatsuit collection and the high-heeled sneakers, both of which have been often copied.

Lycra was no longer confined to use in underwear or swimwear in the 1980s. Knitted single and double jersey is intrinsically elastic and with the addition of Lycra, jersey sportswear could be repeatedly washed and worn, yet still retain its shape. American avant-garde designer Stephen Sprouse set up his own label in 1984, revisiting the 1960s with his skintight DayGlo bodysuits and T-shirts designed in collaboration with Keith Haring.

RIGHT Utilitarian, cheap to manufacture and easy to care for, American designer Norma Kamali propelled gray-marl sweatshirt material into mainstream fashion, as seen here in the oversized jersey tracksuit worn with city bowler and mini legwarmers.

LEFT AND DETAIL RIGHT The spectacular silhouette provided by the unyielding engineering of French designer Herve Leger's "bandage" dress has earned it cult status. The sheath-like dress was first unveiled in 1989, and resembles a series of elasticated bandages wrapped around the torso, allowing Leger to compete with Alaïa for the title "King of Cling."

RIGHT Color-block panels of double jersey are stitched together in this body-con top by Glaswegian-born designer and D. J., Pam Hogg. With a background in fine art, Hogg readily took inspiration from art movements such as, in this case, the Constructivism of Popova.

Deconstruction

Refreshing and invigorating in all this narcissistic display was the work of the Japanese avant-garde. In 1986, Yohji Yamamoto revisited the black turtleneck. Worn with Doc Martin shoes and boots, plus opaque black hosiery, it was a taste of the austere minimalism to come in the next decade.

Challenging the preconceptions of what constitutes "fashion knitwear," the Japanese designers, Rei Kawakubo for Comme des Garçons and Yohji Yamamoto created garments in the tradition of "boro boro," the aesthetic of aged and distressed surfaces, which Americans dubbed "bag-lady chic." Comme des Garçons first showed in Paris in 1982, when their uncompromising approach combined subverting the accepted notion of garment construction with a preoccupation with texture and materials. Garments were cut to disguise rather than reveal the shape of the body and were often derived from traditional workwear in somber hues such as indigo, black, cream and white, with the occasional flashes of red.

Rei Kawakubo's minimalist and austere philosophy appealed to those with an intellectual approach to fashion who deplored the frills and furbelows of 1980s excess. Working primarily in black, dark gray or white, the materials often featured frayed, unfinished hems and an asymmetrical form. In 1982, Kawakubo introduced the black wool sweater of intricate spider's web-like lace, each hole carefully calibrated to sustain the fabric's stability.

Continuing the aesthetic of the Japanese avant-garde were the Antwerp Six, which included Dirk Van Saene, Dries Van Noten, Ann Demeulemeester, Marina Yee and Dirk Bikkembergs. Together with the Belgian designer Martin Margiela, the graduates of the Antwerp Academy deconstructed the accepted notions of knitwear, designing garments with oversize proportions and literally turned garments inside out with linings, seams and hems all on display. Margiela graduated in 1980 and was then a freelance designer for five years. Between 1985 and 1987 he worked for Jean-Paul Gaultier before showing the first collection under his own label in 1989. The first Artisanal collection was produced in the same year at the firm's atelier in Paris. Hand-made from vintage materials, the Artisanal collection is limited in quantity. Inside each garment, the discreet trademark consists of a piece of cloth marked "0." Garments redesigned for men are marked "0+10." The badge is attached to the inside with its four white stitches, exposed to the outside on unlined garments. For the twentieth anniversary the anonymous tag was replaced by a classic logotype. The original Martin Margiela collection eschews the numbered tag for a blank, white label. This is Margiela's primary prêt-à-porter line for women.

French couturier Jean-Paul Gaultier subverted the chunky patterning of Aran knit and its connotations of the healthy outdoors by constructing sweater dresses with conical breasts in 1985. Gaultier frequently utilized this knitting technique and returned to it in 1989 with a seamless evening dress engineered into shape with various stitch patterns, including a twisted cable.

LEFT The chief proselytiser of female underwear worn as outerwear, Jean-Paul Gaultier first introduced the notion and attitude in 1983. Here he subverts the traditional Aran guernsey into a chunky hand-knitted wedding dress with an built-in bra.

RIGHT AND DETAILS

FAR RIGHT Japanese-born designer Junko Koshino deconstructs the indigenous kimono of her birthplace in this knitted wrapover dress. The broad black panel within the patterning of the geometric background signifies the traditional "obi" belt. The scale of the graphic design, in three-color jacquard, indicates that Koshino was an early adopter of the potential of computer-controlled manufacturing equipment that arrived on the market at the beginning of the 1980s.

RIGHT Uncompromising oversized, black lace, roll-neck sweater was manufactured for Comme des Garçons by John Smedley in 1989.

Vivienne Westwood

British designer Vivienne Westwood combines a sense of heritage with the avant-garde, utilizing traditional craft skills to reproduce her iconoclastic ideas. The designer's first collection under her own name was Pirate in 1982. In contrast to the sharp and fitted silhouette then seen on the pages of *Vogue* magazine, the collection referenced a Hollywood version of the high-seas buccaneer through the medium of African-inspired colors and serpentine prints on knitted jersey.

Westwood has always had a provocative, but essentially respectful relationship with the traditions of British craftsmanship. She reinterprets classic designs, uses long-established manufacturing processes and appropriates "indigenous" materials, including Scottish tartans and Yorkshire tweeds, to produce garments that combine meticulous construction and finish with radical design. Born in the small Derbyshire town of Glossop, Westwood revisited her roots when she wanted to ally her avant-garde aesthetic with traditional craftsmanship. Collaborating with Derbyshire knitwear company John Smedley, the designer subverted the notion of the twinset and the historic patterning of the Argyle check to produce her Voyage to Cythera collection in 1989.

John Smedley was founded in 1784 at Lea Mills, Matlock, Derbyshire by Peter Nightingale and his associate, John Smedley. The company is renowned for its fully-fashioned, fine-gauge products in ultra lightweight fine-knit Merino wool and Sea Island cotton. Westwood's collaboration with the company extended to her adoption of the manufacturer's long johns (three pairs of which British mountaineer George Mallory wore for his attempt to climb Everest in 1924), which she decorated with the traditional Argyle check. First used on a sweater for the Duke of Windsor in the 1920s and more usually associated with golf than high fashion, the Argyle design is a pattern of elongated diamonds in two-color intarsia overlaid by a linear check, known in Scotland as "rakers."

Westwood's subversion of the conventional notions of fashionability began in the late 1970s with the Punk revolution. Following the end of the designer's personal and creative partnership with Malcolm McLaren, Westwood produced her epochal Pirate collection under her own label in 1981. She continued to explore innovative approaches to garment construction with her Witches collection in 1983, cutting fabric in the round and on the body rather than on the flat, a process ideally suited to the fluid quality of knitted jersey.

The technique was first used with the much-copied, ripped T-shirt of 1979. This was based on the traditional shape, but instead of the opening being at the neck, Westwood placed it under the arm, allowing the garment to find its own place on the body. To create a three-

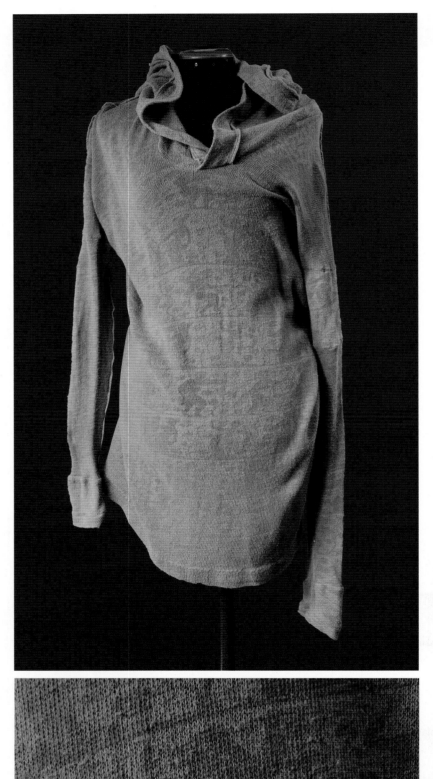

dimensional shape, garments were cut into rectangles with gussets; proportions were altered by cutting the top much higher than the waist. The classic cardigan was made radical by cutting the gray jersey into extremes of shape, extending the sleeves and dropping the shoulderline. Further customization involved appliqué embroidery on the obi-like belt by New York graffiti artist Keith Haring, using fluorescent hieroglyphics.

Although the most memorable knits of the 1980s are probably the oversize crop tops, neon leggings and vivid Lycra of the aerobic era and the signature hand-worked graphic sweaters of Kidman and Krizia at the other extreme, the knitwear manufacturing sector now had the potential for complete free pattern selection, facilitated by the arrival of computerized manufacturing equipment. This, however, remained largely unexploited by designers yet to familiarize themselves with the new technology. When robot machines permitted virtually freehand placement of colors and textures for the first time, manufacturers simply used the technology to create solid, albeit shaped, shade panels. Only in the next decade would the wider potential of these innovations be appreciated, understood and utilized.

OPPOSITE From British designer Vivienne Westwood's 1982 Buffalo Girls collection, this hooded, printed jersey dress combines decorative tone on tone patterning (see detail below), inspired by Peruvian motifs, with an idiosyncratic cut. One sleeve is long and a raglan, the other set-in and of normal length. The success of the collection led to the opening of a shop in London's West End, called Nostalgia of Mud.

LEFT Keen to disassociate herself from the 1970s punk movement, Westwood produced the Pirate collection in 1981, a synthesis of ideas from drawn from seventeenth- and eighteenth-century tailoring and African prints presaged the "pirating" of ideas by Britain's New Romantic movement. This hand-knitted, zip-front, windcheater cardigan is cabled and slashed into a ribbon yoke, with gold trim and a red collar.

ABOVE The 1983–4 Witches collection was designed in collaboration with New York graffiti artist Keith Haring. With a darker, more primitive element, the collection used Haring's Aztec-influenced designs for what Westwood described as "a magical, esoteric sign language." The fine-gauge, wing-sleeved pullover is patterned in two-color rib jacquard, manufactured with new equipment that provided selection for large-scale graphics.

OPPOSITE The sweater with a big heart is designed in intarsia by Vivienne Westwood in collaboration with John Smedley. The deep 1x1 rib was deployed by the designer for a series of fully-fashioned garments, creating a high, defined waist in contrast to the batwing sleeves.

RIGHT Typical of the designer's appropriation of eclectic motifs, Vivienne Westwood's 1989 Voyage to Cythera collection combined references to costumes of the sixteenth-century, Italian improvisational theater *Commedia dell' Arte* and to the work of nineteenth-century French painter Jean-Antoine Watteau.

ABOVE AND RIGHT Bold colors of red, navy, white and turquoise form the foundation for Westwood's Voyage to Cythera collection, manufactured in collaboration with John Smedley. The Argyle intarsia leggings above are constructed from the traditional "long john" pattern from the company archives, dating from the beginning of the twentieth century. The matching fully-fashioned sweater, far right, has a small-check intarsia stripe at the centre front and an embroidered badge of Westwood's "Orb" logo. Also from the same merino wool range, the plain red sweater, right, has been designed with a wide scooped neck and three-quarter-length sleeves.

◀ Body-con dressing
Donna Karan showed her first independent collection in 1985, with the intention of providing smoothly contoured and wearable basics of body-suits, wrap skirts and "bodies" in black and tan stretch fabrics and luxury yarns for the professional woman. Here supermodel Christy Turlington wears a navy wool crepe outfit.

Asymmetry and avant-garde
From Japanese designers such as Rei Kawakubo and Yamamoto came a wave of inventive draping, unraveled edges and "oblique chic" silhouettes, invariably achieved in a minimalist color palette of black, gray and white.

Key looks
of the decade
1980s

▶ Vibrant colors
Despite an extended period when fashion professionals became obsessed with the monochrome gravity of the Japanese designers such as Comme des Garçons, the decade rejoiced in the use of a strong, bright color palettes, as here exemplified by Missoni in multicolor carpet stitch or *punto pellice* fabrics.

Picture knits
Overblown flowers, large-scale animals and classical motifs were worked in colorful intarsia. These graphic picture-knit designs were easily re-created at home by the blossoming number of domestic hand- and machine-knitters.

◀ Oversized sweaters

The 1980s were an era of excess – big hair, big eyebrows and big sweaters. Worn with narrow jersey skirts or leggings the oversize, slouchy sweater emphasized the shoulders and broadened the silhouette. Batwing sleeves and cowlnecks also promoted the top-heavy look.

▶ Cardigan suit

Although Coco Chanel died in 1971, the house continued under the aegis of Karl Lagerfeld from 1983. Here a version of her timeless three-piece cardigan suit is updated by the use of pastel colors, and length of skirt, classic components that appealed to the discerning middle-class, middle-aged consumer of the 1980s.

▲ Multipatterned knits

Japanese designer Kenzo Takada shows his signature miscellany of patterns, weights and textures in his 1984–5, women's ready-to-wear line. The brightly patterned top is strongly influenced by Bolivian textiles – particularly the traditional huipil or woven shirt.

1990s to Now:
Future Collectibles

Technological developments, a second generation of synthetic fibers and a blurring of the boundaries between fashion, sportswear, and art and craft all propelled changes in knitwear design from the 1990s onwards. Innovations such as the "single thread" garment in which the product is knitted in one continuous piece are commonplace. Conversely, artisan effects that result in bespoke one-off pieces, such as the work of Leoney Keogh, have become important components of knitwear design in an environment in which the mass market offers cutting-edge fashion at minimum prices.

Interest in fashion knitwear tends to fluctuate alongside other trends. Garments made from single or double jersey will always have their place in fashion; so sophisticated are some of these pieces that they are perceived as just another fabric rather than a knitted fabric and used accordingly. However, fresh interpretations of the discipline arise as new designers become fascinated with knitwear's potential and versatility. Operating outside mainstream fashion knitwear are the conceptual garments of Comme des Garçons and the work of Jurgen Lehl, a designer who produces knitted pieces celebrating the randomness, variety and irregularity of yarns, together with a concern for sustainability and eco-awareness.

Generally, the pared-down minimalism of the 1990s rendered knitwear, particularly heavy-textured patterned styles, irrelevant. The swing of the style pendulum meant decoration and excessive embellishment were also outmoded. Turkish designer Rifat Ozbek changed the fashion silhouette overnight with his 1990 all-white New Age collection that reflected a new spiritual awareness. Even further removed from 1980s excess was the "grunge" aesthetic propounded by American designer Marc Jacobs under the Perry Ellis label in 1993. Although commercially unsuccessful, it encouraged a whole generation to embrace "dressing down," an aesthetic in which designers such as Anna Sui and Xuly Bet also colluded.

The avant-garde continued to subvert the stitch with implicit sexual overtones as cutting-edge designers such as Turkish-born Hussein Chalayan's Scents of Tempests collection in 1997–8 displayed a sweater with a slit mask in the rollneck that covered the face, while Gareth Pugh featured knitted "gimp" suits in 2005. At the end of the decade designers Alexander McQueen, with his Overlook collection, and Yohji Yamamoto both experimented with notions of extreme scale with hand-knitted garments comprising enormous stitches that altered the proportions of the body.

Technological Developments

The two major manufacturers of flat knitting machines are Stoll of Germany and Japan's Shima Seiki. Both companies have developed CAD pattern-generating systems directly linked to machine production. Electronic control with individual needle selection has resulted in ease of manufacture of complex and sophisticated patterning and shaping that was previously a labor-intensive and expensive process. For some time, machines have been capable of forming panels, shaped internally, rather than just producing pattern pieces.

The two traditional manufacturing cultures of "cut and sew" and "fully fashioned" have blurred, with flat machines producing fashioned and patterned components to attach to other shaped panels from fully-fashioning machines within the same production plant. However, after at least six decades of evolution, there is now another genre of knitwear production equipment at the forefront of new product possibilities. The pursuit of the "integral garment" – and latterly the "whole" or "seamless" garment – has been a saga evidenced mainly via the pages of the trade journals of knitting technology until the late 1990s. As early as 1964, *Hard's Year Book* reported the development of a prototype robotic machine that promised to produce complete knitted shirtwaister dresses without any significant labor cost. However, the astronomical price of the machine, then estimated at $314,200 and translating to millions of dollars today, along with its association with a single moribund style, was the likely reason it never materialized.

Small steps of innovation through the 1970s and 1980s gained momentum in the 1990s from the refinements in digital control of both needle selection and step-motor drive mechanisms. Machines with multiple-needle beds, each with individual needle selection, offered radical possibilities for both the formation and rearrangement of individual stitches and groups of stitches. The usage of this generation of equipment is increasing rapidly and designers are beginning to look to the technology for more than just economies in labor: there are unique aesthetic characteristics that arise from the sensation of wearing garments without seams. As previous generations of machinery come to the point of economic obsolescence they will undoubtedly be replaced with Wholegarment equipment, which is capable of everything previously possible with the additional benefit of highly versatile and seamless production possibilities.

Yarn development has also been a continual vector in the evolution of knitted fabrics and garments, not solely for aesthetic values of texture, color and handle, but also for a variety of performance criteria. The second generation of synthetics following the invention of rayon, Lycra and viscose in the earlier decades of the century include fine polyester, polyamide and viscose fibers, which have become increasingly "smart." These materials are capable of high tensile strength and moisture absorption; they are also responsive to heat and have the ability to insulate. Most importantly, with performance sportswear, the fibers contain "wicking" – the ability to keep the body dry by drawing off moisture. Exploring the limits of materials, fibers such as polyester's slit-film – a type of yarn made by vacuum-sealing a layer of metal such as titanium, chrome or aluminum to a nylon/polyester base membrane, which is then slit into strips for thread – create new avenues for designers. Lyocell, a new cellulose fiber, was invented by Courtauld's in 1988 and given the brand name Tencell.

PAGE 200 With massive visual impact, Alexander McQueen takes the rudiments of finger knitting to catwalk apotheosis in these two ebullient creations from 2000. The sweater uses lightly twisted tops, or sliver, to make an ultra-chunky, reverse plain-stitch bodice with an explosion of twisted and tied hanks, foaming from the neck. The A-line dress has the effect of having been heavily brushed to liberate fibers from the bundles of tops.

BELOW A Wholegarment dress in fine merino wool produced for Intoka by John Smedley. Despite the exaggerated proportions and different structures within the garment, it is produced in a single piece.

LEFT In 2006 John Smedley produced this complex lambswool sweater for the label Intoka, using the Wholegarment technology. Although the puff sleeves are gathered heavily at the cuff and intersect the bodice in a raglan formation, there are no sewn seams: the component panels formed as shaped tubes and "grown" together into a continual three-dimensional piece during the knitting process, which is digitally controlled throughout.

Issey Miyake

Japan-born Issey Miyake is a designer whose constant engagement with textile technology has enabled him to transcend the conventional parameters of fashion. The A-POC (A Piece of Cloth) concept was developed in conjunction with textile engineer Dai Fujiwara in 1999, although it was first shown in knitted cotton and linen stripes in 1976. This is a system of dressing created from one piece of cloth, with no waste and minimum cutting, much like the kimono. With later developments the bolt of cloth was constructed from Raschel-knit tubes: the stocking-like tube is made of double-knit fabric the yarns of which are linked in a fine mesh of chainstitching. If the fabric is cut, the more stretchy fibers in the bottom layer shrink, which tightens the chainstitch mesh and prevents the fabric from unraveling. The cloth was inscribed with pattern pieces that did not require stitching when cut out and could be adjusted by the wearer. The warp knit structure does not "run" and can have openings configured within to accommodate the body and limbs in a variety of optional modes of wearing. This concept has been a recurrent leitmotif within his collections since the turn of this century.

Options included a full-length or three-quarter length dress, with short or three-quarter-length sleeves, a shirt and top, a hood, a drawstring bag, purse, shorts, socks and a water-bottle holder. Attached to the cloth was the date the A-POC was knitted and the adjustment instructions, as was a tiny pair of scissors.

The first customers for the original A-POC generally bought more than one, leaving the other pieces uncut to retain resell value. Since then, the system has undergone refinements and developments: A-POC Eskimo from 1999 included graphic patterning and padding, while the 2000–01 Baguette design relinquished the pattern pieces and could be cut anywhere in the piece.

In 1970, Miyake started his design studio in Tokyo, where he adopted new fabrics such as polyester jersey and the acrylic knit Pewlon. The designer continues to explore and source new fibers and filaments, and experiments constantly with new technology, such as laser-printed fabric, which he uses for reinterpretations of traditional Japanese textile crafts. His 2010 autumn/winter collection, inspired by the mathematician William Thurston's geometric models for the shape of the universe and again in collaboration with Fujiwara, featured layers ropes of knit tubing in cocoon shapes.

BELOW LEFT Issey Miyake takes a pair of scissors to one of his A-POC creations, which – in a single warp-knitted fabric blank – has a variety of pre-constructed garment options. These can be set free from the blank into three-dimensional form by cutting.

BELOW RIGHT The A-POC warp knit concept graphically delineates a complete all-in-one, which swathes the body from toe to headdress in a continual fabric piece.

New Traditions

Current brands and markets have become truly global. In buying vintage knitwear, as with any secondhand product, provenance is important. Designers and brands place bulk orders for more basic knitwear styles in "developing" production areas, while more complex production challenges are given to established manufacturing bases, such as Scotland or Italy, with a long tradition of quality of make. The beginning of the 1990s saw a drop in production by the Scottish knitwear companies: the entire global cashmere clip was bought up by the Chinese, who then produced 100 percent cashmere garments that sold for less than the cost of woollen ones.

An Italian or Scottish cashmere manufacturer would find it difficult to source the raw yarn for their products at the retail price of Chinese-produced garments of the same fiber, regardless of the scale of production. However, this has resulted in the "Made in Scotland" label becoming highly sought after and also insulates traditional brands from unwanted diffusion through association with cheap or even illicit production. The defining styles of an era will reside in the hands of designers who first focus their originality on exclusive products rather than the indiscriminately popular.

The solution to cheap sweaters flooding the market was to look to designers to give added value to the cashmere sweater. British design team Clements Ribeiro was one of the first labels to see the potential in collaborating with traditional manufacturers, initially producing stripy cashmere twinsets and sweaters featuring the Union Jack for the U.K., U.S. and Japanese markets. Following this earlier blip, Scottish cashmere continues to have a greater cachet than knitwear produced anywhere else in the world.

The traditions of classic knitwear have never been more valued, albeit seen from the position of manufacturers repositioning themselves in the context of twenty-first-century high fashion. British heritage labels such as Pringle, Daks, Burberry and John Smedley have understood the need to marry their globally respected quality of make and materials to innovative design, often subverting traditional patterns such as Fair Isle or Argyle for a contemporary relevance. The Burberry Prorsum label of 2009 features a fractured Fair Isle design, the pattern appearing to be worn away on the shoulders. Italian brand Prada also rediscovered the qualities of Shetland yarn in 2009 to produce a range of Shetland oversize cardigans, styled up with wading boots and shorts. Italian company Stefanel – renowned in the 1980s for weekend luxury knits incorporating jacquard designs, stripes and checks – launched a new collection of Fair Isles designed by Annalisa Dunn and Dorothee Hagemann for the brand's fiftieth anniversary in 2010.

Meanwhile, Pringle, now headed by creative director Clare Waight Keller, promotes the ethereal separates of the Scottish brand by featuring the actress Tilda Swinton in a short film by Ryan McGinley, which is set in Scotland. Margaret Howell is only one of the contemporary designers utilizing the skills of John Smedley: currently, the firm is also collaborating with Comme des Garçon. Founded in Scotland in the late 1920s, knitwear manufacturer Ballantyne, known for superb-quality cashmere, worked in conjunction with Central Saint Martin's graduate knitwear designer Louise Goldin to produce a 40-piece capsule collection that combines strong graphic images on innovative programed knits in lightweight jacquard. One of the young contemporary designers to spearhead the knitwear renaissance, Goldin is producing a range of future collectables with her subtle manipulation of fabric and form.

Cashmere Collectables

Donna Karan is so convinced of cashmere's covetability that she has named her latest scent after the noble fiber. Luxe layers are created by the designer's knitwear collections that include heavy-ply ribbed wrist-warmers, draped cardigans with "waterfall" fronts and oversized cashmere ponchos.

Limited quantities always produce a demand greater than the supply, which is then reflected in the vintage value. Queene and Belle, a bespoke knitwear label founded in 2000 by Doreen Keen and Angela Bell, both former head designers at Pringle, combine fashion-led knitwear with artisanal techniques. Garments employ hand-intarsia and embroidery, and the designers use vintage ribbons, lace and beaded motifs for their couture cashmere in a specially-dyed color palette. Every garment has the hand-stitched Queene and Belle logo of a crown and cross.

BELOW LEFT Margaret Howell plays with the proportions of a classic style in 2002. By creating an extra-deep polo collar, tipped with a bright contrast stripe, this fine-gauge sleeveless top becomes a versatile wardrobe staple.

BELOW RIGHT In 2007, Margaret Howell took inspiration from vintage styles of the 1940s and 1950s to fashion this cleverly detailed, fine-gauge top in merino wool. The architectural yoke is defined by carefully matched stripes, which are then echoed by a curved contrast binding around the Peter Pan collar.

OPPOSITE A long, loose cardigan in hand-knitted, chunky cotton, designed by Clare Waight Keller for Pringle of Scotland, 2010. The openwork, cable-striped ground is given substance by the attachment of chains of finger-knitted strips of finer fabric at the sleeve head and front opening.

ABOVE A Louise Goldin diamond-paneled design for Ballantyne, spring/summer 2010.

BELOW FAR LEFT A Margaret Howell cardigan manufactured by John Smedley uses marled yarns and the "false plain" patterning of tweeds. The fully-fashioned cardigan has comfortable proportions, with simple drama attained by the dark contrast of shirt collar and ribs.

LEFT Round-neck merino wool cardigan with set-in sleeves by John Smedley for Margaret Howell in 2003. The bodice is patterned with vertical stripes of Argyle check diamonds produced in intarsia by a Schoeller fully-fashioning, multi-head frame.

The Avant-Garde

An uncompromising approach to knitwear is pursued by radical designers, among them Junya Watanabe, Martin Margiela, Xuly Bet and Shelley Fox. Opposing the culture of newness, novelty and excess, avant-garde designers cultivate the concept of *wabi sabi*, a Japanese term to describe the superior value placed on flawed artifacts through enlightened recognition, first pioneered in the early 1980s by Comme des Garçons. Shelley Fox, internationally recognized as a directional and conceptual designer, used labor-intensive pre-industrial techniques such as felting to produce a distressed surface – a process usually undertaken by mistake and the result of subjecting lambswool to high temperatures and friction to leave a shrunken, solid texture. The designer challenged the precepts of good taste when she degraded the surface of the classic twinset with candlewax, paint and bleach.

Paris-based Belgian designer Martin Margiela deconstructed knitting techniques, choosing humble clothing to cut up and reassemble, such as old army socks partially unpicked and resewn to make sweaters, with the sock heel fitting over the breast and elbows. Margiela has now officially left his own label and Yoox.

com has curated a virtual museum devoted to around 100 one-off pieces by the designer, spanning his collections from 2005 to 2009. Xuly Bet patched, overlocked and embroidered over recycled sweaters, and Bernhard Willhelm embellished his jacquard storybook landscape designs with embroidery. Collecting vintage knitwear by these avant-garde designers is similar to building up a collection of art, which is bought not necessarily for wearability but for its value as museum pieces.

Yohji Yamamoto

Japanese designer Yohji Yamamoto produces some of the most sought-after vintage knitwear. His innovative approach to garment construction, working with the qualities of the yarn that often results in twisted seams and asymmetrical shapes, is instantly identifiable.

Born in Tokyo, Yamamoto graduated from Keio University with a degree in law in 1966. Further studies in fashion design at Bunka Fashion College (Bunka Fukuso Gakuin) led to a degree in 1969. He started designing women's clothing in 1970 and two years later, set up his own company, Y's. His first collection was shown in Tokyo in 1977.

Following his Paris debut of 1981, Yamamoto's influence spread beyond Tokyo. His commercially successful main lines are Yohji Yamamoto and Y's, available at his flagship stores in New York, Paris and Antwerp as well as high-end department stores worldwide. In 2002 Yohji Yamamoto collaborated with fashion brand Adidas resulting in one of the fastest-ever growing brands, Y-3.

Shirin Guild

British-Iranian fashion designer Shirin Guild established her label in 1991, together with her husband, the interior decorator Robin Guild. Completely self-taught apart from a brief period at Central Saint Martin's College of Art and Design, she began designing clothes for herself when she was unable to find items that she liked.

Guild's innovative, minimalistic garments are made of uniquely conceived fabrics, based on yarns from noble fibers such as cashmere, silk, linen, wool, cotton and hemp, as well as stainless steel, copper, hemp, bamboo and paper. Her designs were originally inspired by Iranian peasant clothes and other traditional garments from around the world; they are based on rectangles to hang and drape on the body in a variety of ways. Nevertheless, the oversize, square-shaped pieces acknowledge the proportions of the human form, unlike the work of Martin Margiela: while the width of the garment may be excessive, the sleeves are shortened accordingly. In recent years, the designer's style has evolved to embrace a leaner silhouette.

FAR LEFT A simple knitted tube top by Xuly Bet in 1999, shirred by repetitive stripes of elastic, is made glamorous by the addition of embroidered floral motifs.

LEFT A stripy homespun look by Yamamoto from the prêt-à-porter collection for 1998–99. The baggy jumpsuit and ample, matching poncho dress are hand-knitted in wool and mohair stripes, crowned by wool forms sculpted from dense carpet stitch.

FAR LEFT, BOTTOM Mini-dress with monumental cowl collar in rib-knit mohair from the Maison Martin Margiela autumn/winter 2008-09 collection. Continuing the play of proportions, extra-long textured tights are allowed to fall in gathers at the ankle.

RIGHT A black top with a billowing back and embroidered collar and arm slots was designed by Shelley Fox in 2001. It is teamed with long printed jersey skirt with a black tulle underskirt extension.

The Glamorous Stitch

The association between glamour and knitwear has not always been evident. At most, knitwear has been an adjunct to evening fashions: the cashmere cardigan worn with the taffeta skirt, the beaded top above the velvet trousers. Eveningwear has generally been mediated through luxurious woven fabrics such as silk cut on the bias, folds of duchesse satin and layers of chiffon. However, not only are modern technology and yarns capable of rendering knitwear deluxe, certain designers such as Julien Macdonald have elevated the craft of hand-knitting to embody sophisticated glamour.

Dublin-based designer Lainey Keogh produces exquisite bespoke knitwear in which the yarns themselves are of a paramount importance. Keogh's aesthetic is a very personal expression of mythologies, enabling women to channel their "inner goddess." Discovered by retailer Marianne Gunn O'Connor, owner of the Otokia boutique and Dublin's leading designer at the time, Keogh began designing in 1987 but did not show in London until 1997, when her exquisitely feminine knitwear was critically acclaimed.

Tim Ryan, also Irish-born but now located in London, produces sexy and glamorous knitwear with a rock-chick chic: ripped knit tanks and figure-hugging second-skin minidresses that flash bare skin through strategically-placed holes. Ryan is one of the designers spearheading a reappraisal of knitwear in contemporary fashion, respecting the fundamentals of the craft while intent on utilizing the looped stitch to push the boundaries of fashion knitwear. The designer has a particular fascination with one-piece cutting, attempting to use as few pattern pieces as possible, which often results in seamless garments. Construction and shape are his primary objectives, using integral shaping or single-seamed spiral pieces all constructed from one thread. Ryan only sources the finest cashmeres from Scotland and Italy and all pieces are made in Europe.

Canadian-born Mark Fast was at the center of a media furor about his deployment of three "plus-size" models on the catwalk of his 2010 show at London Fashion Week. Intricately crafted, Fast's clothes appear to best advantage on a curvy body when the garment takes its shape from the person inside it, rather than a structured silhouette being imposed. A graduate of Central Saint Martin's in London, Fast is also in the process of designing a range for British retailer Topshop.

Voyage

A strict members-only door policy was the remit of Louise and Tiziano Mazilli, designer-owners of the London boutique Voyage, which opened on the Fulham Road in the early 1990s. Offering a bohemian look totally at odds with the structured clothes of the time, the garments were exquisite in detail and fashioned from luxurious fabrics with an antique quality. The hand-dyed silk and cashmere, and embellished cardigans with velvet braid and marabou feathers had the fragility and charm of clothes discovered in some long-forgotten trunk in the attic of a historic house. Prices were commensurate with the bespoke nature of the garments; the label included "Invest in the Original" on later pieces.

The "Voyage" persona implied a sort of esoteric allure and beguiling waywardness, typified by such aficionados as Jemima Khan and the late Paula Yates. The Voyage influence was responsible for the "bo-ho" aesthetic that continued from the mid-1990s until the end of the decade and included the eclectic patterning and embellishment of the work of such designers as Dries Van Noten, Matthew Williamson and the Italian couture house Marni.

LEFT Naomi Campbell wears an outfit by Lainey Keogh at the Brown Thomas Fashion Show at the Point Theatre in Dublin, Ireland, 2003. The dress is an elaborate confection of layers of lacy multicolored threads knitted and stitched into a highly textured surface, trailing wispy fronds of white marabou from the neckline.

OPPOSITE With his autumn/winter 2009–10 knitwear collection, Canadian Mark Fast displays a complete tour de force in the use of simple home-knitting machines – with their versatile, non-continual cam systems – to produce extraordinary, integrally formed garments. Using strong elastic yarn and the labor-intensive method of partial knitting, Fast created lace-paneled, clingy dresses, which attracted considerable additional publicity from his use of "full-size" models.

Julien Macdonald

In 2001, Welsh-born designer Julien Macdonald sent down the catwalk a black knitted minidress with a corsage on the shoulder that was embedded with more than 1,000 hand-cut diamonds. Sponsored by De Beers, the garment was kept under guard during its outing. The designer's near-naked web-like constructions reinvented the knitted dress using a base of heavy nylon filament to construct his glamorous, barely-there, red-carpet numbers.

Following a one-year foundation at Cardiff School of Art and Design, Macdonald went on to study fashion textiles at the University of Brighton, then acquired a post-graduate degree in knitwear at London's Royal College of Art in 1996. After being spotted by Karl Lagerfeld, creative head of Chanel, Macdonald worked for the designer while still at college. A year later, he set up his own company, which debuted at London Fashion Week. His first couture collection for Givenchy was unveiled in July 2001. The severe, all-black designs were a departure from the designer's signature style, but Macdonald soon returned to his effervescent and glamorous aesthetic in subsequent work. The designer was awarded an OBE for services to the fashion industry in 2006.

THIS PAGE London-based designer Julien Macdonald used a rich variety of color, textured yarns, hand-knit structures and beads in an organic evolution of intarsia shapes to form this soft openwork sweater-dress from 1999. The scoop neckline is dramatized on the catwalk by a floating headdress of black ostrich plumes.

OPPOSITE Julien Macdonald attains a bold contrast between strips of fake fur and open lacework bands of knitting in this long, funnel-necked negligee coat, which has been constructed on a hand-operated machine.

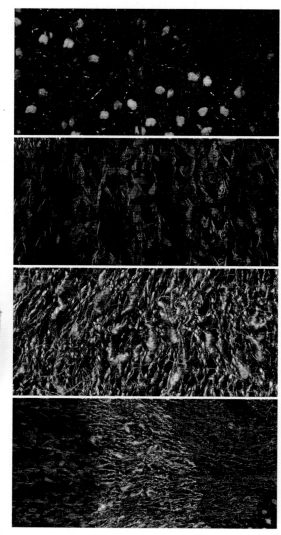

Bella Freud

Introduced in 1990, British designer Bella Freud's knitwear line has all the idiosyncrasy and wit of her fashion label. The great-granddaughter of the psychoanalyst Sigmund Freud and the daughter of the painter Lucian Freud (who designed her logo), Bella is now part of the London fashion establishment. Freud's involvement with British fashion began in 1977 when, at the age of 16, she was offered a job by Vivienne Westwood at her World's End store, then called Seditionaries. Freud subsequently studied fashion in Rome at the Accademia di Costume e di Moda, followed by tailoring at the Istituto Mariotti. She completed her training under Vivienne Westwood from 1980–83 before launching her eponymous collection of tailored knitwear. Success and recognition came in October 1991, when she launched a collection at the London Designer Show exhibition for the first time. In the same month she was named Young Innovative Fashion Designer of the Year at the British Fashion Awards ceremony.

In 2000 Freud was invited to design a line for Jaeger in a bid by the company to reposition itself as a contemporary label. Her knitwear continues to display a quirky irreverence, often with literary references. The 2009 collection pays playful homage to the Beat generation with horizontal striped knits with an intarsia dog interrupting the stripes and iconic black sweaters embroidered with the text "Ginsberg is God."

OPPOSITE, CLOCKWISE FROM LEFT Lizzie Jagger, Ingeborga Dapkunaite and Ayesha Dharkar in knitwear designs from spring/summer 2000; Susie Bick modeling a spring/summer 1992 dress design; and Susie Bick in an "Oh!" top from 2010.

TOP Rib-trimmed sweatshirt in pink for the Love Bella Freud label. The detailing of the panels is highlighted by the use of twin-needle flatlock sewing, creating raised welts on the pointed yoke seam and along the join between the rib underarm and the over-arm panel. The word "love" in a retro-1960s font and the heart insignia are printed.

ABOVE "The Last Poets" intarsia sweater dress in superfine merino from 2010.

CENTER Bella Freud uses a fine-gauge, fitted Breton sweater as the vehicle for the embellishment of a dog's head, panting, for her Sex Bella Freud label.

RIGHT Freud's iconic "Ginsberg is God" sweater in superfine merino wool was launched in 2003.

Collecting and Caring for Vintage Knitwear

The most sought-after knitwear is generally that constructed from noble fibers: cashmere, vicuña, silk and mohair (see pages 68–9). The quality of the yarn is also an indication of the standard of make, such as depth of dye and meticulous finishing. However, synthetic yarns have not always been excluded from design-led pieces, particularly those from the 1960s and 1970s, and labels from this period are collected for their unique design rather than for their classic appeal. Patterned knits may have an all-over design, the result of an automatic jacquard machine, or a single motif, in which case they have been manufactured by the intarsia method, and thus would have been more expensive.

BUYING TIPS

Identifying the fiber or yarn of the vintage sweater can be a problem to the uninitiated if the label is no longer in place. Cashmere has a unique feel; to recognize this quality it is worth handling the real thing in shops to appreciate its authenticity. Don't be deceived by exceptionally soft and furry cashmere, this is the result of the use of shorter fibers from factory-farmed Asiatic goats, which is then slackly knitted. This type of cashmere pills really quickly – check under the arms where there is most friction between the sleeve and the body of the garment. Merino wool has a high-quality sheen and flatness, and lambswool a tough resilience. Silk has a particular smell, not exclusively associated with cheap silk. Synthetic fibers vary enormously in quality, even within their type – rayon can be expensive or cheap, for example – and how the garment wears will depend on the quality.

Fully-fashioned sweaters are knitted in the piece and linked together by a series of loops from a single length of yarn. Check the seams of the sweater to ensure that the linking chain isn't broken, as this would mean the entire seam could unravel. With a patterned sweater, check the length of the floats on the inside – if they are too long, they will snag on wear. Knitted structures are elastic, but not forever. An overworn sweater will have stretched irrevocably on the cuffs and ribbed hem, as will a polo- or turtleneck if there is one. With wool garments, cuffs may be resurrected by pinning the welt every ¼ inch (5 mm) and then pulling against them while passing steam through the rib. Cotton tends not to wear well; the fiber does not have the elasticity of wool and can easily sag. Buttons and buttonholes should be reinforced with fabric or grosgrain ribbon to prevent sagging.

Felting is what takes place when the garment has been overwashed and the fibers have clogged together, providing a harsh, inflexible surface. There is no way to retrieve the initial softness, but sometimes felted sweaters can be cut into and redesigned.

Moth holes in a garment may not necessarily deter you from buying a piece of knitwear, depending on their placement and the severity of the attack. Appliquéd lace, jewelry, braid and corsages can all be utilized to cover damage. Holes can be mended, whether caused by moth or by the knitted loop being snagged and broken. Experienced professional mending is expensive, though, and holes larger than the end of a pencil are difficult to treat as individual stitches must be picked up by hand to reconstruct the rows, matching the tension of the knit.

SAFEGUARDING AGAINST MOTHS

Never introduce a piece of vintage knitwear into your wardrobe without treating it for moths, even if there is no overt evidence of moth activity. It is impossible to tell with the naked eye if the eggs have already been laid. There are three common clothes' moths, and of those, one is prevalent: the webbing moth (*Tineola bisselliella*). It is fairly small (¼ in/5 mm long) and a golden caramel color. It's not the adult moths that do the damage, but the young caterpillars. They will munch their way eagerly through the fibers of knitted fabrics to leave a characteristic scattering of small holes. Generally, you won't see the adults in winter, but if houses are kept constantly above 68°F (20°C), moths will reproduce all year round (otherwise they only do so twice a year). The most common moths in the U.S. are the webbing moth and the case-bearing moth (*Tinea pellionella*).

Moths are particularly attracted to knitted fabrics, as woven fibers are more tightly-wound than those in knitting, making the surface more resistant to burrowing grubs. The softer and more luxurious the yarn, the cosier they seem to find it. At normal room temperature the time between eggs being laid and hatching is a week to ten days, so the damage can happen quite quickly.

- No stage of a moth's life cycle can withstand laundering or dry cleaning, so before packing anything away, dry clean or wash it first.
- Store your knitwear in cotton breathable washable garment bags, unless it is cashmere, then store in a box lined with acid-free tissue paper (see page 216).
- If you can't clean the item, seal it in a plastic bag and place it in the freezer. A temperature of -18 to -25°F (-28 to -32°C) is ideal for seven to ten days. This will kill any eggs that you can't see.
- Moth are attracted to body oils, sweat and stains, so never store a dirty or worn garment.
- Use moth deterrents and change them regularly, at least every three months.
- Cedarwood products can be placed on hangers or in drawers to repel moths. Revitalize the smell by sanding them lightly and add more cedarwood oil.

OPPOSITE A white mohair–wool sweater by American designer Jane Irwill, 1963. Best known for their sweaters, the Jane Irwill Company was started in 1923 and produced classic and fashion sweaters, sometimes with co-ordinates. In the mid 1960s, the company collaborated with fashion designer Donald Brooks.

STORING KNITWEAR

To maintain shape, knitwear should always be stored folded, never hung. Place everything in garment bags and then hang moth deterrents. Do not store your clothes in a hot or damp loft or cellar.

Do not keep cashmere in plastic as this particular fabric needs to be able to breathe. If you have several folded cashmere items, you can use a storage box lined with acid-free tissue. You can also store cashmere sweaters in an old cotton pillowcase but make sure: (a) there are no holes and (b) it is sealed. The best store option for cashmere care is to place your storage box or bag in a spare room on top of a cupboard, not jammed underneath a bed. Never place a once-worn sweater in a bag: you'll only come back to it four months later to find that it has been eaten.

Keep cupboards clean by vacuuming the insides. Remember, a vacuum bag is heaven for hatching moths so be careful to change the bag frequently or put plastic wrap over the nozzle between sessions.

LAUNDERING KNITWEAR

Most manufacturers recommend dry-cleaning as a first option, but always check the label. If there is no label in your vintage item knitwear, play it safe and have the garment dry-cleaned; although some silk, and rayon, can be hand-washed, depending on its quality, others require dry cleaning.

Dry-cleaning

Dry-clean sparingly, such as once a season, as over-exposure to chemicals can degrade the fiber and give a "glazed" appearance.

Handwashing

For handwashing, use water no more than 104°F (40°C) in temperature and a mild detergent. If you are using powder or soap flakes, ensure they have fully dissolved. Turn the garment inside-out to protect the outer surface and soak for about five minutes to help loosen the dirt before gently squeezing. Never rub. Rinse thoroughly in warm water, follow by a cold-water rinse, and use a fabric softener if you wish. Reshape the garment and dry flat (see also page 110).

Handwashing Cashmere

Cashmere aficionados know that careful washing rather then dry cleaning is better for the fiber and maintains the requisite softness. Throughout the process of knitting, the cashmere fiber is hard to the touch because of its oiled finish. During the manufacturing process the sweater is knitted with the yarn in its oiled state and then the sweater is washed in the piece. With experience you can tell if cashmere has been treated to the point of optimum softness. Rough handwashing takes the softening process too far, resulting in shrinkage and felting.

ABOVE A 1950s cardigan featuring a dog motif and checkerboard patterning.

OPPOSITE A chunky knit by Alexander McQueen from his 1999–2000 Overlook collection. Inspired by Stanley Kubrick's 1980 film *The Shining*, the show environment was an arctic, frozen tundra with a blizzard of snow and ice contained within a plexiglass cube.

- Wash your cashmere garment in lukewarm water using a mild detergent.
- When washing by hand, squeeze the suds gently through the fabric – do not rub, wring or stretch it in any way. Then rinse carefully in clean lukewarm water (more than once) until all the detergent has been removed and the water runs clear.
- Soaking wet cashmere knitwear should only be lifted after the excess water has been squeezed out, otherwise the garment could stretch if you are not careful.
- Once your cashmere has been washed, smooth it back into its original shape and place flat on a towel. Dry naturally away from direct heat.
- Never hang your cashmere on a line to dry – it will stretch out of shape.
- Do not tumble dry cashmere unless this is specified as an option on the care label.
- When the garment is dry, press lightly with a cool iron to remove any creases.

Machine-washing

Only machine-wash knitwear if recommended on the label. Use a machine-washable wool setting, a mild detergent and a gentle cool cycle. Avoid biological detergents as they may adversely affect the wool quality. Turn the garment inside out to protect the outer surface.

Drying and Pressing

Dried properly, knitwear shouldn't need ironing at all. If creased, a light press with a cloth between the iron and fabric might be necessary. Dry away from heat, never on a radiator, in front of an open fire or in direct sunlight.

MAINTAINING APPEARANCE

Rest wool between wearings for 24 hours to allow the fibers to spring back and preserve its natural resilience.

- When mending vintage knitwear, never use a cotton thread on a woollen sweater.
- When storing knitwear flat, stuff the sleeves with a roll of acid-proof tissue paper to prevent knife edges on the garment.
- A professional steamer can be used effectively on knitted garments, as it restores texture and does not flatten the surface.

Pilling

This occurs with the entanglement of fibers during washing, cleaning or in wear, so forming balls or pills which stand proud of the fabric, usually under the arms where there is most friction. It is not a fault of the quality of the garment, but the inevitable response of fine fibers to wear. De-pilling devices such as a cashmere comb can be used on the surface of the knit to remove bobbles. Once you have removed the pilling, the cashmere garment will increase in softness and the bobbles decrease over time.

Museums and Collections

UNITED KINGDOM

Fashion Museum

Assembly Rooms

Bennett Street

Bath BA1 2QH

Tel: 01225 477173

Email: fashion_bookings@
bathnes.gov.uk Website: www.
museumofcostume.co.uk

All types of fashion, including knitwear, from the eighteenth century to the present day; includes the complete archive of Sarah Dallas.

The Fashion and Textile Museum

83 Bermondsey Street

London SE1 3XF

Tel: 020 7407 8664

Email: info@ftmlondon.org

Website: www.ftmlondon.org

Founded by Zandra Rhodes. Showcases the best of vintage and modern fashion and textiles with rotating exhibitions.

Gallery of Costume

Platt Hall, Rusholme

Manchester M14 5LL

Tel: 0161 224 5217

Website: www.manchestergalleries.org

One of Britain's largest collections of clothing and accessories: from the seventeenth century to the present day.

National Museum of Costume

Shambellie House, New Abbey

Dumfries, Scotland DG2 8HG

Tel: 0131 247 4030

Email: info@nms.ac.uk

Website: www.nms.ac.uk

A fascinating look at fashion and social etiquette from the 1850s to the 1950s; includes the complete Jean Muir archive.

Victoria and Albert Museum

Cromwell Road

London SW7 2RL

Tel: 020 7942 2000

Email: vanda@vam.ac.uk

Website: www.vam.ac.uk

Fashion and textile collection from the seventeenth century to the present with an emphasis on European design. Features the work of Missoni and Ritva Ross, among others.

UNITED STATES

Cornell Costume and Textile Collection

Department of Textiles and Apparel

Cornell University

Ithaca, NY 14853-4401

Tel: 607 255 2235

Email: caj7@cornell.edu

Website: www.human.cornell.edu/che/fsad/cctc.cfm

A collection of more than 900,000 items from the eighteenth century to the present, a selection of which are on public display.

The Costume Institute

The Metropolitan Museum of Art

1000 Fifth Avenue

New York, NY 100280-0198

Tel: 212 535 7710

Email: thecostumeinstitute@
metmuseum.org

Website: www.metmuseum.org

Vast collection of 80,000 costumes including knitwear from Rudi Gernreich and the Miyake Design Studio Collective.

The Kent State University Museum

PO Box 5190

Rockwell Hall

Kent, OH 44242-0001

Tel: 330 672 3450

Email: museum@kent.edu

Website: www.kent.edu/museum

Collection of mainly twentieth-century garments, representing the work of American and European designers.

Luther College

700 College Drive

Decorah, Iowa 52101

Tel: 563 387 1111 or 800 458 8437

Email: www.@luther.edu

Examples of Norwegian knitting as well as other cultural artifacts can be found at the Vesterheim Norwegian-American Museum here.

Ohio Knitting Mills

4701 Perkins Avenue

Cleveland, OH 44103

Tel: 216 272 6375

Email: harry@ohioknittingmills.com

Website: www.ohioknittingmills.com

A vast collection of remarkable design artifacts from the 1940s to the 1970s.

CANADA

Costume Museum of Canada

109 Pacific Avenue

Downtown Exchange District

Winnipeg

Tel: 204 989 0072

Email: info@costumemuseum.org

Website: www.costumemuseum.com

Clothing and textile collection with over 35,000 artifacts that spans three centuries; includes designs by Coco Chanel, Paco Rabanne, Madeleine Vionnet and Norman Hartnell. Periodicals and books from 1900 onwards and clothing patterns.

AUSTRALIA

Powerhouse Museum

500 Harris Street Ultimo

PO Box K346

Haymarket

Sydney

New South Wales 1238

Tel: 61 2 9217 0111

Website: www. powerhousemuseum.com

Diverse collection encompassing fashion, design, history, decorative arts and more. Contemporary fashion, icons, styles and trends are among the featured exhibitions.

ITALY

Galleria Carla Sozzani

Corso Como 10

20154 Milano

Italy

Tel: 39 02.653531

Email: galleria@galleriacarlasozzani.org

Website: www.galleriacarlasozzani.org

Photography, fashion, design and contemporary art.

Musei Provinciali di Gorizia

Borgo Castello

34170 Gorizia

Görz (Friuli-Venezia Giulia)

Italy

Tel: 0481 533926

Email: musei@provincia.gorizia.it

Website: www.provincia.gorizia.it

The textile section of the museum displays yarns, textiles, fine woven fabrics and garments from the nineteenth century.

FRANCE

Musée de la Mode et du Textile

107 Rue de Rivoli

75001 Paris, France

Tel: (01) 44 55 5750

Website: www.lesartsdecoratifs.fr

A vast collection of fashion and textiles from the seventh century onwards; also features the work of great designers including Christian Dior, Jeanne Lanvin, Alaïa, Pierre Balmain and Christian Lacroix.

Stores and Boutiques

UNITED KINGDOM

Appleby

95 Westbourne Park Villas

London W2 5ED

Tel: 020 722 7772

Email: jane@applebyvintage.com

Website: www.applebyvintage.com

Friendly and accommodating vintage boutique run by Jane Appleby.

Ballantyne London Vintage Store

303 Westbourne Grove

London W11

Tel: 020 7243 9277

Website: www. ballantyne.it

Established in 1921, this prestigious and legendary brand has always relied on the best possible, quality natural fibers. The shop is dedicated to the most refined of cashmere intarsia knits from Ballantyne's historical archives.

Blackout II

51 Endell Street

Covent Garden

London WC2H 9AJ

Tel: 020 7240 5006

Email: clothing@blackout2.com

Website: www.blackout2.com

Affordable, high-end vintage fashion: specializes in clothing from the 1920s to the 1980s.

Cenci

4 Nettlefold Place

London SE27 OJW

Tel: 020 8766 8564

Email: info@cenci.co.uk

Website: www.cenci.co.uk

Vintage fashion and accessories from the 1930s onwards.

C20 Vintage Fashion
Email: enquiries@c20vintagefashion.
co.uk
Website: www.c20vintagefashion.co.uk
Cleo and Mark Butterfield's
inspirational vintage garments are
available for hire. Thousands of
garments – many of museum quality –
including couture and designer.

John Smedley Limited
Lea Mills
Matlock
Derbyshire DE4 5AG
www.johnsmedley.com
Also at:
24 Brook Street
Mayfair. London WIK 5DG

Lyle & Scott Ltd
Ettrick Riverside
Dunsdale Road
Selkirk, Scotland TD7 5EB
Tel: 01750 724239
Website: www.lyleandscott.com
Drawing heavily on subculture, indie
and modernist principles, the Vintage
range is as bold as it is confident.

Missoni
193 Sloane Street
London SW1X 9QX
Tel: 020 7823 1910
Email: boutique@missoni.co.uk
Website: www.missoni.com
Family-run company at the forefront
of Italian fashion since Tai and
Rosita Missoni began creating their
innovative and conventional knits in
the basement of their home in 1953.

One of a Kind
253 Portobello Road
London W11 1LR
Tel: 020 7792 5284
Vintage designer clothing with pieces
from the 1920s to 1980s: labels
include Christian Dior, Gucci and YSL.

Palette London
21 Canonbury Lane
London N1 2AS
Tel: 020 7 288 7428
Email: sales@palette-london.com
Website: www.palette-london.com
Eclectic mix of vintage clothing and
accessories; also a finder service.

Pop Boutique
6 Monmouth Street
London WC2H 9HB
Tel: 020 7497 5262
Website: www.pop-boutique.com
1960s, 1970s and 1980s originals as
well as its own retro Pop label.

Pringle of Scotland
141 Sloane Street
London SW1X 9AY
Tel: 020 7529 1660
Website: www.pringlescotland.com
Founded in 1815 by Robert Pringle,
the company became one of the first
luxury knitwear brands in the world.

Rellik
8 Golborne Road
London W10 5NW
Tel: 020 8962 0089
Website: www.relliklondon.co.uk
Clothing and accessories from the
1920s to mid-1980s.

Rokit
42 Shelton Street
London WC2H 9HZ
Tel: 020 7836 6547
www.rokit.co.uk
Vintage and retro clothing from the
1920s to the 1980s.

The Vintage Clothing Company
36 Stephensons Way
Formby. Merseyside L37 8EG
Tel: 01704 834 403
Website:
www.vintageclothingcompany.com
Extensive range of vintage clothing.

Virginia
98 Portland Road
London W11 4LQ
Tel: 020 7727 9908
Exquisite antique clothing.

UNITED STATES
Annie Cream Cheese of Las Vegas
3327 Las Vegas Boulevard
Las Vegas, NV 89109
Tel: 702 452 9600
Website:
www.anniecreamcheese.com
High-end designer vintage boutique
with pieces from Chanel, Gernreich,
Missoni, Halston, Pucci and more.

Decades Two
8214 Melrose Ave
Los Angeles, CA 90046
Tel: 323 655 1960
Email: info@decadestwo.com
Website: www.decadestwo.com
High-end vintage couture boutique
with a carefully edited selection of
vintage designs from the 1930s
to the 1990s.

Keni Valenti Retro-Couture
155 West 29th Street
Third floor, Room C5
New York, NY 10001
Tel: 917 686 9553
Website: www.kenivalenti.com

The Paper Bag Princess
8818 Olympic Boulevard
Beverly Hills CA 90211
Tel: 310 385 9036
Website:
www.thepaperbagprincess.com

CANADA
Deluxe Junk Company
310 Cordova Street
Vancouver
British Columbia V6B 1E8
Tel: 604 685 4871
Email: dlxjunk@telus.net
Website: www.deluxejunk.com
Vancouver's oldest vintage clothing
store. Great selection of vintage
clothing and accessories.

MaryAnn Harris
Ottawa Antique Market
1179 Bank Street
Ottawa, Ontario
Tel: 613 720 9242
Email: reclectica@gmail.com
Website: www.deluxejunk.com

AUSTRALIA
Rokit
Metcalfe Arcade
80–84 George Street
The Rocks
Sydney
Australia
Tel: (02) 9247 1332
Email: rokit@rokit.com.au
Website: www.rokit.com.au
Large range of fine antique and
vintage clothing.

Vintage Clothing Shop
7 St James Arcade
80 Castlereagh Street
Sydney 2000
Tel: (02) 9238 0090
Website:
www.thevintageclothingshop.com
Eclectic selection of quality original
vintage clothing and accessories.

Organizations
Costume Society
www.costumesociety.org.uk
The society includes collectors,
curators, designers, lecturers,
students and informed enthusiasts
with the aim to explore all aspects
of clothing history.

Costume Society of America
www.costumesocietyamerica.com
Dedicated to the history and
conservation of dress adornment and to
interpreting culture through appearance.

Vintage Fashion Guild
Website: www.vintagefashionguild.org
Online resource set up by a collective
of vintage sellers. Offers information,
news and a virtual museum, plus
guidance for vintage vendors.

Online stores
www.anothertimevintageapparel.com
www.catspajamas.com
ww.chelsea-girl.com
www.dandelionvintage.com
www.davenportandco.com
www.fashiondig.com
www.fevervintage.com
www.thefrock.com
www.hemlockvintage.com
www.heyviv.com
www.miamibeachvintage.com
www.midcenturychic.com
www.tias.com/stores/decades
www.unique-vintage.com
www.vintageblues.com
www.vintagegladrags.com
www.vintagemartini.com
www.vintagetextile.com
www.vintagetrends.com
www.vintagevixen.com

Index

Figures in italics indicate captions.

Further Reading

Age of Extremes: The Short Twentieth Century 1914–1991, Eric Hobsbawn, Michael Joseph, 1994.

Bill Gibb: Fashion and Fantasy, Iain R Webb, V&A Publications, 2008.

Boutique: A 1960s Cultural Phenomenon, Marnie Fogg, Mitchell Beazley, 2003.

Chanel and Her World: Friends, Fashion and Fame, Edmonde Charles-Roux, Weidenfeld & Nicolson, 1982.

Coco: The Life and Love of Gabrielle Chanel, Frances Kennett, Victor Gollancz Ltd, 1980.

Costume and Fashion: A Concise History, James Laver, Thames & Hudson, 1969.

Fashion, Christopher Breward, Oxford University Press, 2003.

Fashion at the Edge: Spectacle, Modernity and Deathliness, Caroline Evans, Yale University Press, 2003.

The Fashion Conspiracy: A Remarkable Journey through the Empires of Fashion, Nicholas Coleridge, Heinemann, 1988.

Foale and Tuffin: The Sixties, a Decade in Fashion, Iain R Webb, Antique Collector's Club, 2009.

A History of Hand Knitting, Richard Rutt, Batsford Ltd, 1987.

Hollywood Knits, Bill Gibb, Pavilion Books, 1987.

Knit One, Purl One: Historic and Contemporary Knitting from the Victoria & Albert's Collection, Frances Hinchcliffe, V & A Publications, 1979.

Knitting Fashions of the 1940s: Styles, Patterns and History, Jane Waller, The Crowood Press, 2006.

Knitwear in Fashion, Sandy Black, Thames & Hudson, 2002.

Modern Times, Peter York, William Heinemann Ltd, 1984.

New York Fashion: The Evolution of American Style, Caroline Rennolds Milbank, Harry N Abrams, 1989.

Norwegian Handknits: Heirloom Designs from the Vesterheim Museum, Sue Flanders and Janine Kosel, Voyageur Press, 2009.

Pringle of Scotland: And the Hawick Knitwear Story, Hugh Barty-King, Quiller Press, 2006.

Scottish Knitting: Shire Album 164, Helen Bennett, Shire Publications, 1986.

Shocking!: The Art and Fashion of Elsa Schiaparelli, Dilys E Blum, Philadelphia Museum of Art, Yale University Press, 2004.

Sportswear in Vogue since 1910, Charlie Lee-Potter, Condé Nast Publications, 1984.

Street Style: British Design in the 1980s, Catherine McDermott, Rizzoli, 1987.

Tennis Fashion, Diane Elisabeth Poirier, Assouline, 2003.

Textile Terms and Definitions, The Textile Institute, 1991.

The World of Missoni, Isa Tutino Vercelloni, Abbeville Press, 1995.

Acknowledgments

Author's Acknowledgments

Special thanks to Lisa Dyer, Lucy Coley and Jenny Meredith at Carlton Books. I am particularly grateful to Dawne Stubbs and Jackie Turner of John Smedley who have been wonderfully helpful, and to Allan Hutchings for his expert photography. Thanks also Jo Hoon, Dr. Philippa Woodcock, Pam Hemmings, John Angus of the University of Derby for his technical input, Steven Tatar of the Ohio Knitting Mills, and to Linda Wood for her archive material. Finally, thanks for the continual and loving support from my daughter Emily.

Publisher's Acknowledgments

The publishers would especially like to thank the following: Mark and Cleo Butterfield for allowing their superb collection of knitwear to be photographed for the book, Steven Philips at Rellik for the Vivienne Westwood pieces on pages 194–5, John Smedley for access to their archive and Kaffe Fassett for writing the foreword to the book. For their help with images, we would also like to thank Missoni, Ballantyne, the Ohio Knitting Mills, Bella Freud, Meg Swansen, Patricia Roberts and Susan Duckworth. Many thanks also go to the photographer Allan Hutchings for the images that appear on pages 34, 35, 36, 64, 65, 75 tr & br, 80, 81l, 100, 125, 170b, 187, 193b, 196, 197c & b, 202, 204, 205bl.

Picture Credits